2~

JAZZ LIVES

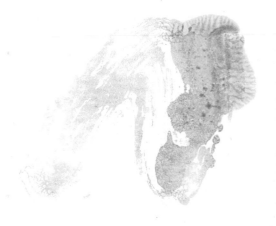

PORTRAITS IN WORDS AND PICTURES

MICHAEL ULLMAN

A Perigee Book

Perigee Books
are published by
G. P. Putnam's Sons
200 Madison Avenue
New York, New York 10016

First Perigee printing, 1982
Printed in the United States of America

Library of Congress Cataloging in Publication Data

Ullman, Michael,
    Jazz lives.

    Reprint. Originally published: Washington, D.C. :
New Republic Books, 1980.
    Discography: p.
    1. Jazz music. 2. Jazz musicians. I. Title.
ML3506.U44 1982   785.42   82-10219
ISBN 0-399-50687-X   AACR2

To My Parents

Acknowledgements

For several years I have been able to publish regularly in *The New Republic* magazine, and I thank Martin Peretz for that privilege and the readers of *The New Republic* for their comments, suggestions and support. For their careful editing and encouragement, I am indebted to Joan Tapper and Roger Rosenblatt, formerly with New Republic Books and *The New Republic*, and Marc Granetz and Jack Beatty, current editors. Closer to home, I thank my friends Glenda Hobbs and William Youngren for their invaluable criticism of many of these essays, and for what they have taught me, often by example, about writing. Patty Davis helped transcribe the interviews on which the book is based. *Jazz Lives* would have been impossible without the genial cooperation of the musicians involved; less obvious are the contributions of their publicists, including Helene and Marty Cann of Rasa Artists, Terri Hinte of Fantasy Records, Peter Keepnews of CBS, Barbara Shelley of Arista Records, Andrew Sussman of Inner City Records, and John Snyder and Maxine Gregg. I thank Leonard Feather for certain corrections in the text. My wife, Harriet Bowdish Ullman, has helped with every step on this project.

Versions of some of these essays have been published in *The New Republic*, *Boston Magazine*, *Metropolis*, *The Boston Phoenix*, and *The Real Paper*.

CONTENTS

JAZZ LIVES

INTRODUCTION

Jazz is a peculiar art form. Once essentially a folk music, it developed in ways no one fully understands out of the music and the culture of southern black people. It has been often called America's most important indigenous art form, and yet most jazz musicians have to scramble to make a dubious living from it. It is essentially an improvised music, yet some of its most important performances have been wholly composed, like Duke Ellington's "Koko" or some of the works of Charles Mingus, Jelly Roll Morton, or Anthony Braxton. It is usually a group music, and yet it depends more than any other form on individual style and individual performance. It is tied closely to the changing conditions of black culture in America, and yet historically jazz as a commercial product has been manipulated and promoted largely by white businessmen, sometimes dedicated like John Hammond and George Wein, but often irresponsible or uncaring.

The life of the jazz player and his music is often subject to the whims of the producers as well as to the changing tastes of the public. Sometimes the system has worked well for a musician. When Louis Armstrong decided to come north to Chicago in 1924, an older and wiser friend advised that he get a white man to handle his business. Armstrong did, of course, and was lucky or charming enough to make manager Joe Glaser a personal friend. Satchmo told this story on the David Frost show, and Frost was shocked that the trumpeter would admit to such a thing. Armstrong appealed to the studio band, saying that they would understand: things hadn't changed that much. Armstrong was willing to turn the business of his life over to others in order to keep his music intact. When he died, the ironies of this life were dramatized. The funeral arrangements were handled by publicity agents. When the body was laid out, thousands of people flowed by, but there was no music: that, it was thought, would be undignified. The funeral was held in Armstrong's own neighborhood, a black, middle-class area of Queens; the people Armstrong had chosen to live with, however, were pushed aside so that dignitaries such as John Lindsay, David Frost and Nelson Rockefeller could enter the church to hear Peggy Lee sing The Lord's Prayer.

The other world-famous jazzman developed a public style even more impermeable than that of Louis Armstrong. Duke Ellington had his own language of staged affection: "Thank you very much, ladies and gentlemen, you're very beautiful, very sweet, very generous, and we *do* love you madly." He also had a ritualized greeting: a feigned kiss on the cheek that made him look as though he were a French dignitary awarding medals. At a White House birthday party for the pianist, Ellington kissed Richard Nixon four times, announcing to the puzzled President that there was one for each cheek. By the end of his distinguished career Ellington would keep the audiences happy by playing long medleys of his most popular tunes, ignoring the groans of his critics and the boredom of his musicians.

If the most famous jazz musicians have to worry about retaining control of their music or about guarding their gifts against the fitful adulation they may receive, the others have to deal with the extensive disregard of the public. Rock musicians make more money and classical musicians have more status. It is no wonder that jazz players are not even happy about the name "jazz," a term with obscene origins, a label that implies to many people a harsh, uncompromising music that will not sell. Jazz, it is argued, is a music of a minority of listeners, black and white, heard rarely on radio and almost never seen on television.

Not only avant-garde musicians have objected to the term "jazz," although as usual they have been most vocal in their protests. Louis Armstrong never tired of repeating that there were only two kinds of music to him, good and bad. When, in a filmed interview, Edward R. Murrow capped a series of surprisingly foolish questions with a request that Satchmo distinguish between "gut-bucket" and "boogie-woogie," Armstrong replied that he didn't know, but that they were both "rhythmatical." The great bass player and composer Charles Mingus asked that his music be called simply that: music. In his autobiography, Ellington claims to have stopped using the term "jazz" in 1943, although the reason for that oddly precise date will always be a mystery. Younger musicians tend to stress the "blackness" of the phenomenon of jazz: the Art Ensemble of Chicago calls its infrequent performances "Great Black Music."

In the little more than half a century of its existence, jazz has changed enormously; there is no assurance that a lover of the swing of the '30s would recognize the innovations of Ornette Coleman even as music, let alone as a valid extension of the tradition. People brought up on Miles Davis's classic performances of the '50s often cannot stand his rock-oriented work of the '60s. Listeners who came to believe that jazz was an intuitive music, born of hard times and heartache and played instinctively by simple souls, will resist having their fantasies disturbed by conservatory-trained musicians influenced by Schoenberg.

Sometimes the harshest critics of the latest "new wave" of jazz are the innovators of yesterday. Many attacked Charlie Parker's tone when he began playing, never thinking that he intended it to have that hard edge. The swing trombonist Jack Teagarden heard the greatest tenor player of our day, Sonny Rollins, and asserted that Rollins didn't know how to play. The same was said about Ornette Coleman, and recently the bebopping alto saxophonist Phil Woods complained that Anthony Braxton, the alto star of the '70s, doesn't know his instrument. Mary Lou Williams, a great pianist and composer herself, was once reduced to the absurdity of telling the world that the greatest pianist-composer of the '50s, Thelonious Monk, used to be able to play before he developed his characteristic style.

Newer musicians can be equally intolerant of previous sounds. Swing pianist Teddy Wilson does a fantastic parody of the square-rhythmed Dixieland piano on a piece called "Moldy Fig Stomp," and Thelonious Monk makes stride piano seem equally hilarious. After listening to one of the great Jelly Roll Morton performances of the '20s, Coleman Hawkins said simply: "All that Dixieland sounds alike to me." These reactions are not inevitable, however. At a jazz and blues festival in Ann Arbor that featured country and urban blues musicians as well as several avant-garde jazz groups, I observed a group of Chicago blues musicians standing at the side of the stage, fascinated with the performance of the Art Ensemble of Chicago. Later, Lester Bowie, the Ensemble's trumpet player, recorded a kidding version of the Louis Armstrong hit, "Hello Dolly." He also recalled a serious childhood fantasy. When learning the trumpet, Bowie heard that King Oliver discovered Louis Armstrong by chance on the streets of New Orleans. With this story in mind, the young Bowie started to play the blues out of the window of his home in St. Louis, hoping rather fondly that Satchmo himself might pass nearby and discover him too.

Bowie is only one of many younger musicians who identify with the whole tradition of jazz but whose creations struggle under the rubric "avant-garde." These musicians' motives are attacked by those who misunderstand their music. Pianist Cecil Taylor, a major force in avant-garde jazz for over a decade, speaks with exasperation of the time when listeners accused him of insincerity in his musicmaking:

It must occur finally to someone that not only are these people serious, but that there is no other way open to them. Because, Jesus, if this is a materialistic society and you're a member of the so-called avant-garde (they even have a little category which means that you're even more exclusively a minority inside a minority), it means you have nothing. You don't even have what passes for communion from your musical community, you don't even have that.

Cecil Taylor says that avant-garde jazz is what it is because its creators had nowhere else to go musically. Leroi Jones compared the new music of the '60s, as played by Ornette Coleman, Taylor and others, to bebop: "Both utilized the same general methods: getting the music back to its initial rhythmic impetuses and away from the attempts at rhythmic regularity and melodic predictability that the '30s and the '50s had laid on it." Bebop and the avant-garde jazz of the '60s and '70s were responses to stagnation, Jones suggests, responses necessary in a music based traditionally on improvisation and innovation. In the '30s, the big band sound, with its square, evenly rendered four beats, dominated the popular music scene. Charlie Parker, Dizzy Gillespie, Bud Powell and Thelonious Monk helped create a new music by subdividing the beat, by writing peculiar musical lines, strikingly harmonized and accented irregularly, and by playing virtuoso solos against a newly liberated rhythmic pulse. Originally viewed as freakish, called "chinese" music by that authority on the Orient, Cab Calloway, bebop is now recognized as a brilliant and authentic creation. The new music of the '60s has not received comparable acceptance, despite the fact that it is another honest response to a musical problem, or set of problems. Charlie Parker himself felt the need for a new development in the music. A master who had revitalized the blues, Parker felt trapped by its form. According to Ross Russell's biography, the saxophonist was at the end of his life searching despondently for a new way to break out of the restrictions of the blues and ballad forms. He talked of studying composition with Edgar Varese, but nothing came of it.

After Bird's death in the middle '50s, jazz seemed to split into a "cool school" of the musicians influenced by classical techniques and "hard bop"—the dominant strain of the late '50s—creations Leroi Jones called unsympathetically mood music for Negro colleges. The hard boppers played a funky, aggressive music, often with references to gospel music and the blues. They tried for soul, while the cool players dabbled in sophistication. Each group created some important and satisfying music, but each style was restrictive in some way. The musicians who were unable to work within these restrictions created the music called variously The New Thing or the avante-garde. Most attempted to free improvisation from the song form, with its recurrent chord patterns, and all stressed new rhythmical patterns and devices.

Throughout the history of jazz, innovators didn't so much close doors as open paths, and today there are inspiring musicians who play in most of the styles the music has isolated and the critics have defined. Even more intriguing, some younger musicians are increasingly interested in reviving techniques and effects of the past. Gunther Schuller wrote of the music of tenor player Ricky Ford, seeing him as typical of a new generation that would use the traditions of jazz:

> I think the young musicians like Ricky Ford are saying in their music: "Hey, let's do this all over again." For they have savored the freedom of "free jazz"; they have learned from Coltrane's extensive and impassioned explorations into the world of modal music; they have readopted bop where Charlie Parker left it twenty-odd years ago; they have had their ears opened by all manner of nonjazz influences (ethnic music, "classical" contemporary music, etc.); and they have, with their ears full of these sounds, hooked up somewhere before the split between rock and the jazz vanguard nearly destroyed jazz. They seem to

be traversing some of the same routes, but with a better understanding of the past, of the mistakes of some of their immediate predecessors, and above all with a profound comprehension that a music cannot isolate itself for very long and survive. Ricky Ford's music is neither narrow nor isolated; it is satisfied with neither yesteryear's avant-garde cliches nor the financial blandishments of today's jazz rock. It is solidly rooted in the past; its heart is big; its ears are wide-open, and so is its mind. It is more than a revival—it is an important new beginning.

One can rejoice in Schuller's prediction of a jazz renaissance without sharing totally his deliberately vague rejection of the music of the immediate past. Jazz is a serious music, "as serious as your life," as McCoy Tyner told Valerie Wilmer. While the music has changed, it still requires the dedication and discipline of its musicians; few of them can expect the solid financial rewards or public renown their talents deserve. The musicians I have written about in this book have played New Orleans style, Dixieland, swing, bebop, Latin, and some highly sophisticated contemporary styles. Some can play all these musics. There are odd connections amongst them: jazz violinist Joe Venuti, famous since the '20s, and Anthony Braxton, a controversial avant-gardist, are the two musicians most affected by classical traditions, while Doc Cheatham, who improvised on trumpet before he knew jazz existed, played in Latin bands during the same period that hand drummer Ray Mantilla was learning his trade.

These musicians have shared a common problem: how to survive as artists playing jazz, a music that is still appreciated by only a minority of Americans. The essays that follow document the innovative responses of some accomplished musicians to the conditions under which they live. Joe Venuti's career began in the '20s. He used his learning and instincts to play popular and classical music as well as jazz. After traveling with several bands, Neal Hefti settled in California to work in the television and film studios. Tommy Flanagan accompanied Ella Fitzgerald for a decade, while Horace Silver has managed to lead groups and record for over twenty-five years. Ken McIntyre, Karl Berger and Ran Blake are all respected educators: the first two have Ph.D.s, an indication of the sophistication of a growing number of jazz musicians who have learned to support and promote themselves in unexpected ways. Two musicians—Betty Carter and Marian McPartland—successfully started their own record companies when larger organizations refused to record them. Unable to practice and perform regularly in New York City, Sam Rivers opened the Studio Rivbea in his home; the studio became a mecca for young musicians migrating to New York.

Still thought of as a music that depends on group interaction, jazz is today more than ever a *recorded* music: as fewer musicians can find steady work as players, their recordings become more important. I have therefore included essays on two record producers interested in preserving jazz; John Snyder and Steve Backer have very different ideas about the role of record companies in supporting the music. Musicians as "entertainers" have at times struggled against the lingering Puritanism of some of our institutions, as my essay on Max Cohen and the cabaret card case suggests. While there are few jazz musicians competently managed, managers are still important to the business, and Maxine Gregg talks about what a manager can do. Jazz musicians have had bad reputations: few people would want their daughter to marry a jazz musician and, as Marian McPartland observed, even fewer would want their daughter to become one. That too is changing. The charm, modesty and seriousness of the musicians I have described are most seductive. Jazz musicians are no longer primitive, if they ever were: as Sam Rivers told me, merely intuitive musicians now fall by the wayside. I have spoken to some of the finest of those who have survived, and their insights into their music, their lives and our society form the core of this book.

JOE VENUTI

Jazz violinist Joe Venuti died on August 15, 1978, ending a professional career that began in 1919. Venuti had been in the spotlight since 1924, when he was hired by Jean Goldkette, billed then as the Paul Whiteman of the West: it was the Goldkette band of 1927, with Bix Beiderbecke, Frank Trumbauer and Venuti, that Rex Stewart called "without question the greatest in the world and the first original white swing band in jazz history." Venuti was, Stewart added, "the premier jazz violinist of the day." Fifty years later the same could have been said of this vigorous, accomplished man.

A masterful self-publicist, Venuti presented Leonard Feather with the attractive tale that he was born in 1904 on the ship that brought his immigrant parents to this country. When confronted with this story, a relative of Venuti's is said to have commented, "Yeah, and he was playing pretty good at the time, too." Venuti was the only person I've met old enough to drink who liked to exaggerate his age: he was once visibly chagrined at Dick Gibson's Colorado Jazz Party when informed that Eubie Blake, now in his mid-nineties, was going to attend: Venuti liked the distinction of being the oldest musician there. A short man of variable girth, Venuti dressed impeccably in the style of a successful elderly businessman. He had a large bald head, an expressive wrinkled face and powerful wrists. He practiced an hour and a half a day to maintain his reflexes. Tough to the end, typically he had a smile on his face and a glint in his eye.

He told interviewers Shapiro and Hentoff about his early training: "I think a cousin started to teach me when I was about four. Solfeggio, of course. That's the Italian system under which you don't bother much about any special instrument until you know all the fundamentals of music. It's the only way to learn music right. Later, when I started to study fiddle seriously, I had several good teachers. I even put in six years in a conservatory" (*Hear Me Talkin' To Ya*).

Venuti's father wanted his talented son to become a classical violinist, another Paganini. Joe's classical training was rigorous: when I asked him about it, he responded by crossing himself and looking towards the heavens. He said that his father did not take his crossover into popular music lightly, knocking Joe about the head every time the youngster began to swing. Hired by Goldkette, Venuti was suddenly making a lot of money, and like a dutiful son, he sent much of it home to Philadelphia. His suspicious father chased him down, but it was too late to change Joe Venuti's ways, and anyway, the old man was relieved his son wasn't stealing the money.

Joe Venuti went to school in Philadelphia with Eddie Lang, born Salvatore Massaro, one of the first great jazz guitarists. (Not only did Lang influence Django Reinhardt, but he made blues recordings under the pseudonym Blind Willie Dunn.) Venuti played with Lang until the latter's death following an unnecessary tonsillectomy in 1933. As young boys, Venuti and Lang learned to improvise together; not by playing jazz, but by working out impromptu variations on the Italian tunes the boys performed at dances. Venuti recalls those days in *Hear Me Talkin' To Ya*: "You know, Eddie and I went all through grammar school and high school together. We used to play a lot of mazurkas and polkas. Just for fun we started to play them in 4/4. I guess we just liked the rhythm of the guitar. Then we started to slip in some improvised passages. I'd slip

Joe Venuti *by Michael Ullman*

something in. Eddie would pick it up with a variation. Then I'd come back with a variation. We'd just sit there and knock each other out."

Until Lang died in 1933, he and Venuti were almost inseparable, recording with the Goldkette and Whiteman bands and with groups of their own. Their classical skills were useful in dance tunes and light classics, and their precocious ability to swing their more stolid mates was one of the dependable attractions of these bands. The famous Joe Venuti Blue Four recorded a gently swinging "Apple Blossoms." It begins as Venuti states the melody, drifting effortlessly into harmonics at the end of a phrase, demonstrating his superb technique without the strutting show-time effects common to the earliest jazz virtuosos. It is performances like these which, according to Richard Hadlock, "represent a pioneer effort to present chamber jazz with a minimum of unmusical effects or superfluous vocals and without any pretense of its being anything but music for *listening*" (*Jazz Masters of the Twenties*). The Venuti-Lang groups often feature Adrian Rollini on bass sax and Arthur Schutt, Frank Signorelli or Rube Bloom on piano, but they rarely include a drummer. The Venuti-Lang experiments that began as variations on popular dances eventually helped take jazz out of its accompanist role.

No gentle tune can illustrate the most characteristic Venuti playing. The 1931 version of "After You've Gone," recorded with Benny Goodman and Jack Teagarden, features a relaxed vocal by Teagarden that demonstrates the influence of Louis Armstrong in its trumpet style phrasing, vocal smears and tumbling decrescendos. After this vocal, the piece moves into doubletime and Venuti takes over authoritatively, flinging dramatic phrases at top volume over a background that is suddenly enlivened. A critic has aptly dubbed Venuti's music "hard swing." No Venuti phrase is without its heavy accents and powerful thrust, but most contain arch turns and rhythmic oddities. He liked to surprise, which he did sometimes by playing a straight version of Dvorak's *Humoresque* in the middle of a jazz set, or by building surprises into his solos. A recent version of "Sweet Georgia Brown," performed with guitarist George Barnes, begins with some harmless noodling on the violin that just barely suggests the tune. Venuti then repeats some patterned rhythmic phrases that are traded off with Barnes. Joe continues to tantalize the audience with what is obviously an introduction until suddenly he leaps into an up-tempo, jived-up statement of the infectious melody. After his accompanists' solos, Joe comes back to trade phrases, and he finishes by riffing as if he were a whole big band. Most of Venuti's up-tempo performances ended with this kind of playing, which was meant to contrast with the long, single-note phrases of his improvisations. The zestfulness of this solo was typical of Venuti: he was a formidable competitor as well as an inspiring accompanist. In his 1975 performance at the Newport in New York Festival, Venuti performed with Vic Dickenson, Earl Hines, Red Norvo and others, tipping his bow at each to tell him when to solo, and saving the final spot for himself. He blew them all away with "Sweet Georgia Brown."

Famous as he was for his music, Venuti was once more well known for his pranks. The late Bing Crosby experienced both Joe's music and his wit. In his autobiography, *Call Me Lucky*, Bing says of the former: "High on my personal list of memorable moments are the great duets of Joe Venuti and Eddie Lang." But Joe's personality clearly made Bing a little wary. Crosby devotes most of a chapter to Venuti's practical jokes, which included throwing a piano out of a third-story window to find out its basic note: no one agreed, so all bets were off. When Red Nichols, the owner of the piano, protested, Venuti asked him what he was complaining about, since he had gotten his five bucks back. Bing describes the young Venuti in this way: "Joe's a voluble, volatile, and violent Italian. He's very loud, very noisy, and very given to telling fantastic stories about himself and his family. . . Joe likes everything with *beaucoup* volume. He told me once he would have liked to have been a tympanist but if he had, he would have had to use hatchets for whatever a tympanist uses for drumsticks." The hatchet image, nonsensical as it is, suggests that the softspoken crooner was intimidated.

Venuti could flare up even in old age, but only once did he light a whole stage on fire: he was offended when a Cincinnati country club owner refused to heat his dance hall adequately. Venuti liked to insist on his rights. Boston disc jockey Tony Cennamo tells the story about a visit with Venuti to an Italian restaurant in Boston's North End. Before they entered, Venuti complained that maitre d's never look a man in the eye. His companions scoffed until they entered the restaurant, when Venuti won his point by glaring like a basilisk at the hapless host, who immediately looked away.

Venuti stayed around Seattle for much of the '60s, combatting alcoholism. That struggle won, he emerged in the '70s with a sort of second career, recording on five or six labels with musicians such as Marian McPartland, Zoot Sims and Dave McKenna, appearing at Newport All Star occasions, and touring with various small bands. Whitney Balliett wrote movingly of an impromptu duet that developed between Venuti and Sims: "Each man solos with exhilarating fervor, and the two go into a long series of four-bar exchanges in which Sims plays astonishingly hot and funny parodic figures. The final ensemble, jammed as hard as any collective improvised passage I have ever heard, is unique, for the two instruments are so close tonally and melodically and rhythmically that they sound like one instrument split in half and at war with itself. The number ends, and Ira Gitler, an editor of *Down Beat*, appropriately shouts, 'Jazz ecstasy' " (*Ecstasy at the Onion*).

Venuti was a hero to many. Spiegle Wilcox, a trombonist who played with Joe in the Jean Goldkette Orchestra in the late '20s, showed up at engagement after engagement of Venuti's last years, buttonholing members of the audience to tell them how great Joe really was. When Wilcox took a chorus on trombone,

Venuti stood beside him smiling benevolently, obviously thinking it wonderful that someone Wilcox's age could even make a sound. Venuti's recorded works offer a unique opportunity for jazz historians: one can, for instance, compare two of his solos on the tune "Dinah," one recorded in 1973 with Marian McPartland and the other in 1926 with Jean Goldkette.

Venuti retained his sense of humor. At Sandy's Jazz Revival, a club in Beverley, Massachusetts, owner Sandy Berman asked Joe to tell a few stories to the audience. Venuti proceeded to talk of the night his manager came to Sandy's, said hello and explained who he was. "Four dollars," Sandy replied. Having told his tale, Venuti played a couple dripping choruses of the sentimental ballad, "What Are You Doing For the Rest of Your Life," pausing in the middle of a phrase to repeat "four dollars." At odd times for the rest of the evening, Venuti got his revenge by holding up four fingers or by mouthing "four dollars," and pointing at the imperturbable club owner. Venuti was not one to let an advantage pass. Like Davy Crockett, he could out-talk, out-eat, out-drink and presumably out-wrestle any man he came across. And he played up a storm.

DOC CHEATHAM

When Doc Cheatham plays, he tilts his head way back, places his trumpet firmly against his lips and spreads his arms so wide that his elbows are close to shoulder height—he looks like a dignified elderly version of the reveille-blowing bugler once popular in sentimental movies about boys' camps. Adolphus Cheatham has been playing the blues and jazz since the '20s when, as an adolescent in Nashville, he first heard rare recordings of such new style trumpeters as Johnny Dunn. A flexible, refined player with a warm but restrained tone, Cheatham has rarely been out of the music business since he hit Chicago in 1926. As a relatively unsophisticated youngster who was teaching himself to read music, Cheatham studied trumpet players: his early heroes naturally included Louis Armstrong but also Arthur Whetsol, a star with the Duke Ellington band, and the sophisticated Bix Beiderbecke as well as the brash Roy Eldridge. Once a lead player for Cab Calloway, McKinney's Cotton-pickers and Benny Carter's band, and often a Dixieland soloist, Doc Cheatham played with Latin bands in the 1950s when bop and rhythm and blues made unpopular the melodic, older style of jazz. Cheatham nevertheless counts several bop trumpet players among his favorites: Fats Navarro, Clifford Brown and Clark Terry, all known for beautiful sound as well as for agility and harmonic sophistication. Although "the money has never been forthcoming," Cheatham looks on the vagaries of his long career without rancor. He's had a lot of experience, he says, and most of it has been fun.

Cheatham was born in Nashville in 1905. He taught himself both trumpet and saxophone, tutored only by the leader of a neighborhood children's band. "I just picked up the trumpet. I didn't have any schooling. We had a juvenile band there in the neighborhood church, organized for kids, and we got some old secondhand instruments. We weren't playing jazz. We were playing church music and marches mostly. They wouldn't allow us to play any jazz in church, but we'd sneak and play it anyway. We'd play anything but what they wanted us to play. That was the way it started." Jazz came relatively late to Cheatham's home town: "In Nashville we had no way of listening to any jazz, other than the very few records that were coming out. There weren't too many of those, but we had bands come through there with shows." In his teens, Cheatham started to sit in the pit of those vaudeville theaters, playing only for the experience: "We had a lot of bands coming up and that's the only way we could hear them."

At the same time, Cheatham was playing school dates. "We were playing dance music, you know, because Nashville was a school town and we had a lot of school dances. There was an old bar there. I used to go up and play with the piano player—play by ear. Called ourselves playing 'jazz.' For me it was the beginning of jazz, because I didn't know anything before that time. I think in Louisiana they were doing it way before that. We didn't have too many jazz players in Nashville. Our piano player was a barber. He couldn't play but one or two tunes, but he could play the blues. He knew the blues. They always knew the blues. I don't know where they got it from."

At Nashville's Bijou Theater Cheatham accompanied the great blues singers: "That was on the TOBA circuit. They had a circuit starting from Atlanta all the

Doc Cheatham *by Michael Ullman*

way up to Chicago and back all through the southern states and midwest. I played for all the blues singers. The greatest for me, though, was Clara Smith. The blues singers in those days, the people who'd listen to them were what we called a lower class of people; the elite people looked down on blues singers. Because Nashville was a school town, everybody was so dignified that blues singers had a rough time drawing an audience other than the rough element. They would pack the theater to hear the blues. Clara Smith wasn't an educated type of person—very rough and mean— and those are the better blues singers than the educated type of performer. Clara made up her own lyrics and the lower people who came to hear her appreciated her because she spoke their language. Clara was down, really down. The gutter type of blues singer. Bessie was a little more refined."

Cheatham left Nashville for the first time almost by chance. "I was playing in the pit of the theater—not being paid—and a band came through there with a show with one of the kids who was in the Our Gang comedies. They called him Sunshine Sammy; he was about the only black kid in the comedies. He could sing, he could dance, he could clown. So his father took him on a tour. They came through Nashville, and they heard me playing and they engaged me. I went on the road with that show. The show broke up because there were money problems and I joined other shows out there on the road. From one show to another, I ended up back in Nashville. A man came through by the name of Marion Hardy—The Alabamians—and they engaged me as a cornet player. They broke up and I wound up in Chicago. I stayed in Chicago in 1926 and bummed around there."

Excited by the talent in Chicago and interested in improving his playing, Cheatham set out to study the trumpeters around him: "I always tried to be a good musician and a good player and I got some pretty little gigs with Louis Armstrong's wife and other people. I've always studied trumpet players. I've always wanted to play like the best that I could hear, and by being interested in the horn and in music, I taught myself a lot about harmony." While clearly Cheatham learned something about phrasing from Armstrong, he doesn't project the power underlying Armstrong's style. His urbane, almost reflective playing owes something perhaps to another early influence, Arthur Whetsol, lead player with the Duke Ellington band until incapacitated by alcoholism, a musician known for his sweet but unsentimental tone.

"I like Arthur Whetsol very much. I copied a lot of his things, and I wanted to play like him. The New Orleans trumpet players always fascinated me. All of them had some different style that comes from the individual— some type of feeling for jazz—and I learned something from all of them. I made it my life study to listen to all those players. They were all inspiring to me."

Since the '20s Cheatham has admired individualistic innovators like Roy Eldridge and Bix Beiderbecke: "Roy was tearing up Chicago at that time and he is still a great trumpet player. I was never able to play that type of jazz that Roy plays because he's an individualist like Buck Clayton. Buck Clayton was a great player. Bix brought a new idea to jazz: his style and his knowledge of his instrument, of the different variations of harmony and chord changes. His improvisation on melodies was something that no one else did. No one else played like Bix. During those years jazz was being created. Every time you'd hear a good player, it was something new. They sprang out and they're still coming. Improvement—I think it's all improvement in jazz."

Although he was excited by the music in Chicago, Cheatham soon realized that he was getting nowhere financially: he left for Philadelphia and Bobby Lee's Cottonpickers. "Philadelphia was a very fast city— jazz bands all over the place. So I worked with the Cottonpickers in Seagirt Inn in New Jersey until the seasonal thing slowed down there. I didn't care to work in the honky-tonks, because it was just a matter of everybody drinking and getting drunk and running around and staying up all night, and I don't like that. I had an offer to go to Wilber deParis's band—a better band than I ever played with before. Wilber was a man of many talents, and he always wanted to be a great band leader." When that band failed, Cheatham went on to New York City. "I played around New York for a while with a band—gigging and playing theaters. At the time they had a lot of acts—dance acts, singers, and naturally they had a band. We played the Keith Circuit until the band petered out. Then I bummed around here and worked with Chick Webb's band. That was before he became famous. Then Sam Wooding, who had a great band in Europe, came to New York for a rest. He picked me up and took me to Europe with him." Cheatham was to record with Wooding in Barcelona in July 1929, helping out on the vocal of a song named "Carrie." He could even arrange for the orchestra when necessary: "I did a lot of arranging for Sam, and then I got to the point where I stopped doing that because there were so many writers and arrangers; I devoted my time to the trumpet, instead of fooling around writing and carrying on."

In 1930, after a recording session in Paris with the Wooding band, Cheatham returned to New York, first for a return engagement with Marion Hardy's Alabamians, then for a time with McKinney's Cotton-pickers, until he finally took a job as lead trumpeter with Cab Calloway's orchestra. He had been fearful that he wasn't improving abroad. "At that time you couldn't hear anybody in Europe, and it was just a matter of playing just what you know—no competition. I wanted to improve myself, so I left and came back and joined Calloway." Calloway's powerful big band was largely designed to back up his camp vocals, but Cheatham enjoyed the work: "Cab was young and very, very hot then—popular. He was hard-working. We were a good band; we had a few band numbers, real fast. We did a lot of theater work. Later Cab slowed down and he decided to put in better players like Chu Berry and Jonah Jones, Shad Collins, Ben Webster, Eddie Barefield—he changed over quite a few of the men and his band became a great jazz band." Cheatham was playing lead trumpet. "I liked it because at that time the lead trumpet player really swung the whole band. And if the band was with him, he really knew it." But the work meant that Cheatham, a graceful and imaginative soloist, got few spots to himself: "When I left Cab [in 1939] I gave up all the lead trumpet and started doing solo work. I worked with Teddy Wilson's big band, Teddy Hill, Eddie Heywood—jumping from one band to another. I haven't done any lead playing to amount to anything since then."

A healthy, energetic man today, Cheatham had a couple of what he calls "breakdowns" during his big band years. "I broke down with Cab traveling around— a whole collapse of the body systems. Of course, we weren't eating properly. Being on the road jumping around on buses, you don't get a chance to eat properly and you don't sleep right. And I was never a real strong, big healthy guy. I was always a weakling—and I'm very lucky that I'm not dead because I went through a whole lot. I laid off for about two years. In 1945 I was with the post office. Stopped playing. I had another problem; I had a wisdom tooth extracted. The dentist messed up a nerve in my lip, and I was playing at the time at the International on Broadway with a trio. And I couldn't hardly make a note, but the boss said, 'Stay up there anyway,' and the doctor said, 'Keep playing,' and so I kept playing and my lip got all right. I realized at that time, although I hated to stop playing, that I'd better stop and rest. I always managed to take care of myself after that.

"I don't drink. My only problem is I smoke a cigar or pipe once in a while. I kept my teeth in good shape. That's very important for a trumpet player. I think I'm in good shape for my age, pretty good shape. You never know what's going to happen, but I never worry about that. You never know what's right and what's wrong for you half the time. I try very hard to take care of myself and I enjoy playing now more than ever."

Cheatham had made his reputation as a lead trumpet player, but by the '40s the big bands were dying. He was a melodic player, and the inventors of bebop were running chord changes, as they called it. At first Cheatham couldn't understand this new music: "When I first heard it, I didn't like it because I was trained to play around the melody. They also were playing around the melody, but I couldn't hear it. I came up playing the 1-3-5 harmony. Well, they added the 6th or 7th, and now there's the 13th, 14th, 15th and all that stratosphere playing. The bop players could improvise much faster than anybody else. I think sometimes in the beginning it was too fast for the people to comprehend." Nevertheless the bop revolution helped end the big band era. In the late '40s and '50s, Cheatham took part in several of the unsuccessful efforts to revive bands such as Calloway's: "Cab made a comeback with a big band and we almost starved to death. We played places on the road where, if we had competition from a place where they had blues singers and a tenor saxophone moaning and chicks singing the blues—well, they outdrew us and there was no more money. People weren't dancing anymore and the progressive and modern players came in."

Instead Cheatham took jobs with society bands. And unable to play what he called jazz, he was grateful for the chance to work in trumpet sections of top Latin bands. "I played with Latin bands quite a few years, because that was the only thing I could do. I traveled to South America with great bands, because they started down there at that time playing jazz with a Latin beat. There was Machito and there was Ricardo Rey—he had one of the greatest."

The last decade has been fruitful for Cheatham. When he left Rey in Puerto Rico, Cheatham returned to New York to an offer from Red Baliban, who had a Dixieland band in the Village. The '70s saw Doc's return to jazz along with a revival of interest in his music. Cheatham plays with several jazz repertory orchestras dedicated to reviving the music of past masters where his experience with New Orleans blues, with the small jump bands and the big bands of the '30s, as well as his continued prowess as a trumpeter and his personal charm, make him an attractive musician. "That's what's keeping me busy: the knowledge of all those old tunes from the early '20s," he says too modestly.

In the New York Jazz Repertory Company, Cheatham both solos and reads. He travels to European jazz festivals, and plays with various small groups. He is still excited about music, still gaining experience. "Everything that I've done has been an experience that I can look back on and think it has paid off as far as my playing is concerned. I just love what I'm doing now."

It shows in his repertory company performances; when Cheatham moves toward the microphone for a solo, the audiences sit up in anticipation and murmur gratefully. Cheatham's solos are still full of surprises—he can play in the declamatory style typical of Louis Armstrong or use Bix's more coy phrasing. He can play Dixie, swing, or in a style that most listeners would be tempted to call pure music. His ballads such as "I Cover the Waterfront," recorded in 1976, are notable for their rich but effortless renderings of the melodies. On Dixieland tunes Cheatham might choke the end of a phrase using a half-valve technique of Rex Stewart, or follow a bold period with its modest echo: he avoids the artificial bounce and forced cheerfulness of many of the Dixieland revivalists, and he gains through charm what others capture with flair and dramatics.

His one regret is that he has never been given an opportunity to control a recording session: "I have never yet had anyone come to me and say, 'Doc, I want you to make a recording album,' and then leave me alone and let me do what I want to do. In France, I came very close to it, but I still didn't have the right to pick who I wanted on it, to choose the things I wanted to play and the people I wanted to play with." As we finished our talk, Cheatham walked me to the nearest subway station. Few men are heroes to their neighbors, but Doc Cheatham is clearly recognized and admired on his block. He greeted everyone we met, commenting cheerfully on the cabbages one man was selling on a corner, waving graciously to the old people sitting on a park bench. Everyone was glad to see him, but

Cheatham's mind was clearly running on the problems of his theoretical record session. If the chance came up, he would have to decide about the rhythm section—and how could a man with so many musician friends choose among them? In his typically modest and considerate manner, he said: "I'd rather not make the record if I had to hurt anybody's feelings. Because, they're all great friends of mine—and they're all great players. If I thought I was hurting anyone's feelings, I would rather not do it."

That's not the attitude of someone driven to be a star. "I never wanted to be a leader. I don't like that because it's a responsibility. Never wanted that. I just want to go and play. Now everything's coming easy. The money's not coming, but I don't worry too much about that. In music, well, music's something where the music comes first. Unless you're a big shot—like Dizzy or Lionel—but I haven't reached that point yet. I doubt if I ever will, but I'm enjoying what I'm doing. That's all that matters."

MAXWELL COHEN

Maxwell T. Cohen is a New York lawyer and a liberal man. Now in his seventies, he teaches a course called "Perspectives in International Human Rights" at The New School, and in the spring of 1979 he traveled to Russia to help negotiate the release of two Russian families living in the basement of the American Embassy, victims of religious persecution. His 1964 pamphlet, "Race, Creed and Color in Adoption Proceedings," challenged lawyers to combat restrictive laws prohibiting interracial and interreligious adoptions, and his challenge paved the way for opponents of those laws—which were subsequently struck down. Cohen has been connected with jazz musicians since *Ebony* editor Alan Morrison called him to aid Bud Powell, then declared legally incompetent due to mental illness. Cohen has since represented many musicians and entertainers, including Ellington, Dizzy Gillespie, Stan Getz, Nina Simone, Miriam Makeba and Lenny Bruce, and he has defended others. He chaired several seminars given in the palmy days of George Wein's Newport Jazz Festival on subjects such as "Religion and Jazz" and, more importantly, on the problem of drug addiction among musicians.

Cohen's most significant contribution to the lives of jazz musicians, however, came when he began fighting the infamous cabaret card system for licensing entertainers in New York bars and clubs, a procedure used until the mid-60s to prevent artists with police records from performing in New York City: Bud Powell, Frank Sinatra, Charlie Parker and Billie Holiday were among those denied such a card. Insecurely based on law, during its existence the cabaret licensing procedure inevitably became corrupted. It is said that large amounts of cash disappeared within the police department, and musicians still speak of illegal means of procuring the license. One prominent musician told me that when he came to New York City he was instructed by friends that to get a card he only needed to bring a large amount of cash to the executive of a then-prominent record company. Cohen observed this system and attacked it in a series of court hearings until the cabaret card licensing procedure was abolished by the New York City Council. As a result, in 1974 Cohen was one of three non-musicians honored by the Newport Jazz Festival: he was said to have helped more musicians gain employment than any other living man.

I talked to Cohen about his background, about Bud Powell and about the cabaret card hearings. He is a small, neat, zestful man, a native New Yorker, who in the past few years has taken up the cello. We talked in his Riverside Drive apartment. "I was born in an area very much east of Riverside Drive: East Harlem. It was a poor area containing Irish, Italian, Greeks, Jews and probably a smattering of other nationalities. There were four-story tenement houses, four families to a floor, with the toilets in the hallways. We had wood stoves and no hot water. But out of that background in East Harlem came Rodgers of Rodgers and Hammerstein and a number of great musicians, composers and writers. I became a lawyer during the Depression. The standards of acceptance at colleges and law schools were then very low. I did not know at the time whether I wanted to be a lawyer, but the alternative would have been just to wander around without direction. The Depression was bad enough without that, so reluctantly I entered law."

Maxwell Cohen *by Jack Davis*

Known for his championing of liberal causes, Cohen was notified when Bud Powell's legal problems were crippling him unjustly. At the time Cohen did not know Powell, or that he was the preeminent bebop pianist and an important composer. Admired by Art Tatum and emulated by such younger pianists as Al Haig, Hank Jones and Tommy Flanagan, Powell was afflicted throughout his life with spells of mental illness. "Alan Morrison, an editor of *Ebony Magazine*, was very much concerned with jazz and jazz musicians, and I'd known him for several years. He asked me whether I would assist a musician, Buď Powell. Powell had been insane and it is required by law that where a man who is insane has property and property rights an authority should be appointed. The authority has the curious name of The Committee of an Incompetent Person. Powell's Committee, possibly because they did not know who he was, were not handling him properly. They were skeptical of his status as a musician. Incidentally, when he was admitted to Bellevue Hospital, the psychiatrist asked him what he did, and he said he was the composer of over 600 songs. The psychiatrist made a notation that the patient had delusions of grandeur. At the time Bud Powell was competent. I succeeded in having the Committee removed and Powell was permitted for the time to obtain employment as a completely sane and competent individual.

"We became good friends. I could talk to him and appreciate him without gushing or belittling him. We spoke about music frequently. He told me the classical musician who influenced him the most was Debussy: the quote was, 'I dig that cat.' And there was a Debussy quality in some of his work. He was an ungainly pianist, though. Wilson of *The New York Times* admired Bud, but he could never understand how this man who played at the piano with such stiff fingers could perform those incredible arpeggios. John Levy told me about one incident with Powell. At Birdland one night Powell sat down to play the piano. It must have been an extraordinary experience because his musicians stopped. Other musicians came from their dressing rooms to listen. Powell was alone on the stage there under the spotlight, performing away, obviously extemporaneously, with an amazing series of improvisations, transitions, counterpoint melodies. No one had ever heard anything like that, and it is still discussed as one of those phenomenal situations.

"Still, Bud was a sad man. His life was tragic; he had a very unsympathetic mother who had him arrested twice. His brother Richie was killed in an automobile accident. His son almost died, having swallowed medicine by mistake. And his musical inventiveness was so great that his piano was not a sufficient outlet. When we talked there were long periods of silence. He might have had nothing to say and often he had nobody to say it to. But he was not dissociated from reality. He could identify people and he was sufficiently oriented to travel by subway, to be on time, to appear on stage sober, and to perform. Towards the end his appearance on stage was curiously depressing. At Birdland, Pee Wee Marquette would announce, 'Here comes the amazing Bud Powell.' There'd be a lot of applause and Powell would come from left stage, crossing very slowly and perspiring profusely. A sad looking face, even in repose. And suddenly the audience applause would diminish. By the time he got to the piano there would be no more applause.

"After Powell was declared competent he was offered work again at Birdland. He did not accept the job because he did not have a Police Cabaret Identification Card. This was the first time that I knew of the existence of this handicap that kept thousands of musicians and entertainers out of New York. I was incensed that such a law could exist, and I knew it was contrary to the policy of the State of New York because there had been cases that held that rehabilitation was an important factor in granting state and city licenses, and the i.d. card was not a license, nor even authorized by law. The fact that one had once been a criminal was not necessarily damning if evidence could be shown of rehabilitation. So we had a police department ignoring the public policy of the State of New York.

"I later learned that the system got started accidentally. There was around 1939 a Presidential Directive to the FBI instructing them to prepare a list of those whose presence might be adverse to the security of the United States. It was thought that many of the unions were dominated by Communists, particularly the waiters' union. The list was prepared. Later when the police department was helping in an attempt to break a strike, they became involved in passing on the qualifications of waiters and chefs to work in restaurants. If they had any previous criminal offense, even as minors, they could not work. This was seen as a way of weakening the unions. In the course of time, like any other uninhibited authority, this began to stretch horizontally, and in the process it began to take in musicians and performers. And so a 'law' never passed by legislation (and so never intended to restrict musicians and artists) became a tremendous factor in their lives. There was one decision in 1941 that sustained the law and said that the police had the right to such an authority because of the number of cabaret robberies, none of which was committed by musicians or performers. It was an outrageous decision, but it gave some degree of legal coloration to what the police department was doing.

"I knew some of the musicians who were suffering because of the law. The very distinguished J. J. Johnson was denied a card. He had committed an offense as a juvenile delinquent. The law was and is very firm that delinquency can never be a legal disqualification against a man after he became of age. Johnson's was the first test case. It was successful to the extent that the court directed the police department to give him a card. The court avoided the issue of whether the police department had any rights in respect to the establishment of the card as a criterion for employment, but the very fact that the police department had been challenged successfully was important. There were several test cases after that."

The climactic case, according to Cohen, resulted in a

dramatic spectacle. It involved the white comedian and social commentator known as Lord Buckley, a hipster who used the slang of bop incongruously and humorously. When in 1960 he applied for a card, Buckley was asked if he had any previous arrests: he answered no, forgetting he had been picked up for possession of marijuana nineteen years before. Denied a cabaret card, Buckley notified his manager, who engaged Max Cohen. "Lord Buckley was managed by a well-known novelist and former editor of *The Partisan Review* by the name of Doc Humes, Harold Humes. Harold went down to the police department with a tape machine hoping that in the course of arguing for Lord Buckley's card someone would approach him for a bribe. No one did, but the policeman in charge referred to the fact that there was very little difference between a performer and a criminal anyway. That brilliant observation was taped and I made much of it later. Humes introduced me to Buckley at the suggestion of Dorothy Schiff, publisher of *The New York Post*, and I asked the police department for a hearing. Now these hearings were usually before an inspector who was sympathetic. They were simple hearings. I would produce the applicant and he would testify that he was married and that he had not committed an offense for a number of years. In other words, that he was rehabilitated. And that would have been the routine in Lord Buckley's case except that Doc Humes was a very effervescent individual with a tremendous amount of energy and a sense of drama. So instead of one witness he came with eight noted writers and with reporters from the New York papers. It was a Friday afternoon. We didn't finish the testimony, and the hearing was postponed for two weeks. Lord Buckley died one week later. [November 12, 1960.] He died on a Saturday night. Then an amazing thing happened—seventy-eight of the foremost writers and publishers in New York formed a citizen's committee to fight the police department on this issue. The New York papers made this front page news."

The Citizens' Emergency Committee, formed at the

home of George Plimpton, included such figures as Norman Mailer and Norman Podhoretz. The Committee demanded an investigation of the police department, asserting that the fees paid by entertainers were being diverted into the Police Pension Fund. The Committee also stated that certain prominent entertainers were allowed to perform in New York City despite their inability to get a card—within a week Frank Sinatra admitted that he had twice played at the Copacabana without a card. A later investigation turned up over one hundred men and women working in cabarets without the proper license: Sophie Tucker was discovered to be working with an expired card. Humes alleged that there was a list kept by the police department of entertainers allowed to work despite police records. While the list never turned up, Cohen charged that Lord Buckley had been asked to pay a bribe in order to obtain his license.

The hearing took place on November 14, the same day Mayor Wagner ordered a sweeping investigation of the police department. The session, held at the police department's Division of Licenses in Worth Street, was described by The New York Times as "one of the stormiest ever conducted." Surprisingly, it was conducted by Police Commissioner Stephen Kennedy, who was both outraged at the idea of an "emergency" in the police department and eager for some publicity. Before the session was over, Kennedy threatened Cohen with action before the bar committee, while Cohen demanded Kennedy's resignation because of his "psychopathic behavior." Cohen noted that Buckley died of a stroke caused by hypertension, adding that the entertainer had not eaten for two days before his death; Kennedy quipped that he should have gone on welfare.

Buckley's family took the position that Buckley was entitled posthumously to a card. "At the scheduled hearing, at which I planned to ask for a card, even posthumously, at the Buckley family's request, I appeared with one witness. When I came to headquarters I was surprised to see a number of television cameras, reporters and high officials in the police department. I was told by the officer in charge [Officer Lent] that the Police Commissioner, Stephen Kennedy, was going to sit in. He was a feared political power, a man who would throw his weight around in the city. During the hearing, which was very simple, the Commissioner handed the Inspector in charge a note. I asked to see it, but the note was torn up. We knew from the Inspector's apologetic demeanor that it instructed the Inspector to deny the card. Then Commissioner Kennedy took over, and began harassing my witness. He asked his name, and then whether the witness was known by any other names. I pounced on the Commissioner. 'You don't have the right to offend a witness by that question.' And then we went at each other as the cameras began to grind. The Commissioner had made a tactical mistake: a powerful individual should not start up with a small man. Later Doc Humes came in and it became a shouting match between the two of them. Finally at about three o'clock we finished." After the hearing, Kennedy acknowledged to the press that he had lost his temper, blaming his behavior on his "Irishness." He did not explain why he took over the hearing in the first place.

On November 21 George Plimpton spoke for the Citizens' Emergency Committee when he said "the cabaret licensing system itself violates constitutional rights and by its very existence breeds corruption." On November 30 a group including Nina Simone and Quincy Jones brought a suit challenging the police's right to require permits and demanded an accounting of over $1 million in licensing fees that were said to have been deposited illegally in the Police Pension Fund.

"That was the beginning of the end of the police card. The unions originally had opposed me—they were afraid of offending the police. Now they were on my side, but the musicians' union fought for the transference of identification cards to the Department of Licenses. I fought that. After I had demonstrated there was no legal basis for the licensing, they were helping to make such a law, this time supervised by the

Department of Licenses. The fight continued until, after a while, the City Council eliminated the entire situation. The tragedy of the police card was of course that it was devastating to the careers of thousands of otherwise qualified and competent performers."

The lives of musicians are somewhat easier as a result of Cohen's efforts. Whatever the private opinions of the police department, now the law makes it impossible officially to equate entertainers with criminals. Soon after the cabaret card case Cohen's law practice changed and he saw fewer musician clients. He didn't forget them, however. He represents several on "a sentimental basis." He emulated them perhaps. At seventy years of age, Cohen took up the cello, and he speaks with delight of the times when, returning from a cello lesson and walking along the streets of New York with his instrument, he was greeted by other musicians. Cohen has not been forgotten by the world of jazz, either. When handed his citation at the Newport Festival, Cohen received a polite hand from the audience. But when he turned to leave the stage the musicians had assembled behind him, he told me proudly. They were applauding, and with fervor.

EARL HINES &
DIZZY GILLESPIE

The evolution of jazz since the '20s has been so rapid that musicians, barely of middle age themselves and having just reached the full maturity of their developing style, often find that style outmoded. In 1943, the thirty-eight-year-old Earl Hines, a highly successful and innovative pianist who had fronted his own big band since he was twenty-seven, found himself working with the pioneers of a new music with new rhythmical and harmonic ideas. At various times during that year Hines's organization included Charlie Parker, trombonist Benny Green, singers Billy Eckstine and Sarah Vaughan, and a thin, bespectacled virtuoso trumpet player and admired clown, John Birks Gillespie, known as "Dizzy." Gillespie would soon be known not only as a leader in a musical revolution, but as a leader in fashion, with his beret, goatee, horn-rimmed glasses and hip talk. It is doubtful that any lovers really courted by whispering "Ooh-Shoo-Bee-Doo-Bee" into each other's ears, but Gillespie's recorded sweet nothings were a definite advance over those of Tin Pan Alley.

Whatever Hines's feelings about this development within his band, the early pairing of Hines and Dizzy Gillespie seems appropriate. "Fatha" Hines and Dizzy are both astonishing virtuosos who extended the techniques of their respective instruments. Each is a consummate musician who has survived the rigors of a long musical career, and who today is creating music as valid and often as exciting as when he was in the vanguard of the jazz tradition. Neither man is particularly successful with a down-home blues, and neither has a typical ballad style. Hines plays ballads with rattling force, while Gillespie eludes their traditional emotional implications with his swallowed notes, bursts of speed and advanced harmonics. Hines and Dizzy both shy away from obvious dramatics and sentimentality. Their styles are marked by an obliquity of approach and a restlessness in execution.

In Hines's case, one should talk of a succession of styles. He has been a professional since the late '20s, and became recognized as the top jazz pianist with a succession of recordings in 1928. In that year he recorded eight inimitable piano solos for a small label that specialized in piano rolls, QRS, and some small band performances with Jimmie Noone, the most polished of New Orleans clarinetists, as well as a group of pieces with Louis Armstrong that remain among the greatest of all jazz recordings. Gunther Schuller and Martin Williams credit the 1928 tune, "West End Blues," with reorienting jazz towards a new emphasis on the solo performer, away from the patterned group improvisations of the New Orleans sound. In keeping with this development, Hines freed the piano from its orchestral style: the left hand would now typically keep the beat, while the right would produce horn-like single note passages, often complete with pauses where a trumpet player would take breaths. But Hines did not stop innovating there. He was not satisfied with the regular thumping of the bass line known as "stride": his bass lines stop eccentrically, and his rhythm has become increasingly free over the years. The melodic lines produced by his right hand have extended themselves. He has now as much of a two-handed style as any pianist, but the effect is rather of a conversation between hands than of a full orchestral style.

These developments may owe something to Hines's

Earl Hines and Ahmed Abdul Malik *by Robert Parent*

early classical training in Chopin and Debussy. He was born in 1905 to a middle-class family of fine musicians in Duquesne, Pennsylvania (*not* known as a center of the blues). The young Hines, more at home with Czerny than with ragtime, decided to go into jazz playing, he said, because it was easier to make a living in jazz than in the classics. That was certainly true for a young, black pianist. In his early twenties, Hines found himslf in Chicago, known as a center of gangsterism but important also as a meeting place for jazz musicians of the midwest and south.

His rise to fame was almost immediate. Hines spent much of the next twenty years leading his own bands (of varying quality), although never with great financial success. After a troubled stint with Louis Armstrong's All Stars in the late '40s, a pairing that produced more personal problems than musical solutions, Hines was forced to play in a Dixieland band in the manner which he had supplanted almost twenty years before. He dropped out of view for a while, but his music was revived by some daring record producers in the mid-60s, when it was discovered he could still produce magnificent solo performances in an elaborate but effective style. Hines became a star and a leader again.

Today, a typical Hines solo might open with an understated theme, rendered with something of that rushed, submerged tension which Erroll Garner borrowed from Hines and exaggerated. Hines then moves into a series of variations, each more agitated than the last, until he abruptly halts the regular bass pattern, swirls up and down the keyboard with his right hand, punctuating his runs with savage left hand jabs, ultimately resuming the bass line and engaging in a dramatic conversation between hands. His is a music of grand gestures and magisterial control. Of his recent performances, Hines's solo work is the most satisfying. On tour, he surrounds himself with a group of musicians with impeccable credentials but inferior inventiveness. Recently, the band has included a singer whose cute stage presence, complete with unconvincing wiggles and sopranino squeaks, infects her singing, which is unpardonably affected.

The Hines band that included Dizzy Gillespie never recorded, so we have no example of these two musicians working together. In the early '40s when he was a member of Hines's band, Dizzy was still evolving his style. A two-record set put out as part of the Smithsonian Collection documents this process. Dizzy counts pianists among his early influences, although he does not mention Hines in particular. On the horn, he points to Roy Eldridge, known as Little Jazz, as a major influence, and the Smithsonian Collection shows him moving away from Eldridge into a readily recognizable style of his own.

Roy Eldridge is the first major trumpet stylist after Louis Armstrong. Not having quite the blues feeling of Louis, Eldridge can be just as emotional. Whereas Louis was able to rely on his magnificent tone and spacious, even grandiose, phrasing, Eldridge sacrificed space for speed. He was a young man in a hurry, and his crackling sound with its quick, intense vibrato was perfectly adapted to his rushed rhythmic sense. Eldridge could imitate Louis sincerely (as on "Basin St. Blues"), but when Dizzy Gillespie recreated Satchmo, he produced a grotesque parody of Louis's showboating before a big band: "Pop's Confessing." One cannot expect one ham to like another's act, but Gillespie's parody of Armstrong suggests some unrecognized influences on his own music. The performance emphasizes an aspect of Armstrong's vocal style: his tendency to finish a strongly stated phrase with an offhand comment, running down a scale in a continuing diminuendo. "Confessing" also parodies Armstrong's tendency to exploit solo trumpet breaks for dramatic effect. Both these habits became part of Gillespie's mature trumpet style.

What intervened between Armstrong and Gillespie, and between Eldridge and Gillespie, made the young Gillespie intolerant of the older style. There are new rhythmic ideas, as seen in Gillespie's lightning fast runs with their irregular pauses and accents, and new harmonic ideas, most obvious in his reworkings of such standards and jazz tunes as "How High the Moon" and "Cherokee." This new trumpet style was an appropriate creation for a man of Gillespie's emotional makeup. A wry, witty man, he has always been known as a clown and a showman with a head on his shoulders. Dizzy like a fox, they say about him. All of the wit and some of the irony is present in his music. He avoids the emotionalism of a Roy Eldridge performance and the grandeur of the classic Louis Armstrong. When he plays a spiritual, it becomes "Swing Low, Sweet Cadillac." Gillespie used to end his performances with a chorus of blues on trumpet, followed by a one-syllable parody of a howling blues singer: "Awwww," he'd shout, following the cry with an abrupt "Bye." And that would be that.

Gillespie's great performances are intense, but with a different kind of intensity than that of Eldridge. His power comes from the ideal matching of his active musical intelligence with his great technical skill. He plays faster than Eldridge; he plays faster than virtually anybody. Gillespie is perhaps *the* technician of the trumpet, and he has discovered new sounds with his rapidly articulated half-valve notes and his clever and dramatic use of mutes. Whereas the excitement of an Eldridge performance is that he seems always to be reaching for something almost out of his grasp, the thrill of listening to Gillespie is that he is always in command. Gillespie's rhythmic sense, and the bebopper's stress on fast tempos, make a tone like that of Eldridge impossible for him. In fact, Gillespie was criticized for his thin tone early in his career. But now we can see that every aspect of Gillespie's playing has its attractions. He is not as magnificent as Armstrong, or as heated as Eldridge, but he is a master who has molded a brilliant personal style to the demands of an innovative music.

Both Hines and Gillespie seem to enjoy great physical vitality. It is astonishing to think that Hines made some of his most important records fifty years ago. Anyone who listens to his recent recordings of

Dizzy Gillespie *by Deborah Feingold*

Ellington tunes can hear the joy that is still in his playing. *Dizzy's Party* on Pablo has Gillespie adapting to new dance rhythms: the result will not be to everyone's taste, but it shows that Gillespie is still open and aware. What Dizzy said about himself with uncharacteristic simplicity, is true of Hines too: "I was developing. I am developing." The jazz life that proved dangerous to so many musicians has kept these two young.

NEAL HEFTI

Neal Hefti is a sandy-haired man in his mid-fifties, gracious and articulate. Known to jazz fans for his arrangements and compositions for Woody Herman ("Wildroot" and "The Good Earth") and for his sixty or so pieces for Count Basie, Hefti has also had a distinguished career in popular music, writing and arranging for movies and television, for the Maguire Sisters, Kate Smith, Arthur Godfrey and others. He conducted as well as arranged a famous "strings" session with trumpeter Clifford Brown. "L'il Darlin'," arranged for the Basie band, is his best known jazz piece, but the theme from *Batman* is his most lucrative composition. A man who was brought up in a rich popular musical tradition, Hefti gave up his career as a jazz trumpeter for the more secure life of an arranger-composer in and around Hollywood. He has the unique perspective to justify his distrust of arrangers who are too self-assertive and musicians who don't consider the tastes of their audiences.

Hefti was born in Nebraska to a musical family: "My mother was a piano teacher and she taught all us children how to play piano at an early age, eight or nine, after which we could read the bass and treble clefs and pick an instrument. We also had a family band—not all that big of a money making scheme, but it practiced a lot. It played a few parties and things of that nature." The family band needed brass, so Hefti was given a shiny, second-hand trumpet on Christmas. By the time he was in high school, Hefti was playing in local bands as well as "in what was roughly called the Omaha Symphony," led by Henry Cox. He also started writing and arranging for "territory" or, more derisively, "Mickey Mouse" bands. These dance bands, modeled after the organizations of Guy Lombardo, Kay Kaiser and Sammy Kaye, worked and lived out of buses. In the summers, he played in carnival bands. "The music of the region was what is now Lawrence Welk." It was, as Hefti said, "germane to the territory," despite its "schmaltzy gimmicks and overphrasing." Hefti gave the audience what it wanted, arranging military taps and polkas for a drummer named Franklin Vincent, whose wife had a traveling dance school. For the carnival he wrote some background music for a trapeze artist.

One of six children, Hefti was told by his older brothers that he must go either to New York or Los Angeles to become a professional musician. He went east with a Mickey Mouse band led by Dick Berry. Hefti made it only to New Jersey, though, where he was fired. He spent the next ten years scuffling in New York, hampered, like many other musicians, by the recording bans and musicians' strikes that plagued the industry in the '40s.

In New York City Hefti first became seriously involved in jazz. "I really had to learn jazz"—a music not germane to Omaha. He learned by listening to the Duke Ellington records friends brought to his hotel room. Hefti's first jazz job, still as trumpet player, was with Charlie Barnet, who has "some super arrangers" of his own. Then, in the mid-40s Hefti moved to California with Charlie Spivak's organization. In Los Angeles Hefti worked with Spivak's band for over a year, making a movie, playing in hotels, ballrooms, theaters, and doing some one-nighters. "When the band left, I just didn't want to leave." After some weeks with the Mickey Mouse band of Horace Heidt, Hefti was called by Chubby Jackson to replace

trumpet player Cappy Lewis in the Woody Herman organization. "Shortly after that I started writing. Ralph Burns and I wrote about 90 percent of the book for the next few years."

Herman's band, called later "The First Herd," gave Hefti his first major opportunity as a jazz composer and arranger. The band was in flux as a result of the war and the draft—part of Hefti's appeal to a bandleader was that he was 4-F because of a recent car accident. "This is when the slogan came about, 'Don't shake hands on the bandstand.' So many people were drafted in Woody's band that every night it was almost like a new band sightreading the book. It got to the point that Woody couldn't call out his real swinging numbers. The band couldn't read the existing arrangements. So we started faking." Many of the pieces Hefti helped provide were improvised head arrangements. "That only meant that they weren't written down. They were taught, memorized, made up from the heads of two or three people."

This band played a series of hotel dates, which meant a quiet set at dinner and a louder one at night. Woody would rarely show up for the earlier set, and the members of the band had a lot of freedom. They also had a problem: "We didn't have too much to play without him, because he had the book in which he would either play alto or clarinet or sing on all the good numbers." Hefti tried to fill the gaps. "This is how 'Happiness is a Thing Called Joe' was born. We were stuck for tunes. We had to improvise. If there was a leader at that time, it was Chubby Jackson."

When Hefti married the late Frances Wayne he adapted easily to the supporting role of singer's manager, arranger and accompanist. "Ninety percent of what I learned about the business I learned in the next two or three years with Frances." Hefti was now looking at music from a different perspective, "from the angle before it's presented. From the inception, from the sperm alone, I started visualizing the ultimate product—whether it's right for the person." He was considering not merely the artist, but the audience, simultaneously adapting his arrangements to its tastes and his wife's talents.

Back in New York, Hefti worked with his own band as well as wrote arrangements for whomever was interested. Count Basie was one. "I joined Basie when he was at his lowest. Count Basie had a six-piece band—he was playing all the chicken shacks in New York—what they call the chitlin' circuit . . . They were really scuffling. They were with Columbia Records, and Mitch Miller didn't even want to record them." When Basie got a job playing one tune with a big band at the Apollo, Hefti wrote the tune "Little Pony" as a feature for Wardell Gray.

Hefti takes partial credit for the ensuing success of Basie and his band. "During the '50s he probably recorded sixty pieces of mine, and it brought him from a six-piece band to the Waldorf Astoria to appearing for the Queen." Morris Levey, owner of Birdland and the founder of Roulette Records, offered Basie a steady engagement in his club, and at the same time asked Hefti to write arrangements for a new Basie album. Hesitant at first, Hefti accepted when given what he calls "complete artistic control" over a session that was originally to be called "Basie Plays Hefti." The result of this session was the smash single "Li'l Darlin'." A surprise hit, "Li'l Darlin'" is a slow number, conservatively voiced, featuring an eerie, restrained trumpet solo by Wendell Culley, who alternates shy phrases with long tones permeated by a weird vibrato; the notes sound as if they are coming from the other side of an electric fan.

Hefti attributes his success with Basie to his ability to figure out the Basie sound: "A writer writes for the person. The person does not perform for the writer. Anything we can we throw in to enhance what that person already has—we're not trying to change him at all." Unlike more ambitious, and perhaps less successful arrangers, Hefti started with his own sense of what Basie was: "He's a sort of basic blues piano player. This man's charts were wrong—he was writing for Miles Davis, or he was writing for Duke Ellington.

When Basie himself played the piano solo, it didn't sound like it was part of the overall picture. It sounded like 'what's wrong with this picture' . . . They would write these things with beautiful, exotic harmonies, but when Basie came in with his basic Red Bank or Kansas City blues, it was laughable in comparison." In Hefti's words, their collaborations brought Basie into the daylight; he was no longer the leader of a "creepy undercover group." Daytime disk jockeys were playing his music; he entered the mainstream of American music, an environment in which Hefti is quite comfortable. In his youth Hefti played music that was a part of the community; not surprisingly, he does not "separate jazz and pop." His success with Basie was followed by the stay in the studios of sunlit Los Angeles, where he still resides.

Hefti considers the arranger a musician whose job it is to catch the personality of the person he's working for. The stronger the musical personality of that artist, the easier the task. He was frustrated with his work in 1948-49 with Harry James, because James was "unsure of himself . . . He always vacillated. One day he loved 'You Made Me Love You,' and the next day he hated it. James I couldn't find—but I consider it more his fault than mine." Woody Herman presented a similar problem. "There was no approach to him. He himself didn't have a style that he insisted on. I wrote mostly for the guys in the band." Finding Basie was easy: "He never changed his mind—maybe because he couldn't change his mind . . . but I don't have to find that out."

Given Hefti's assumptions that the arranger must find the "truth" of an artist, not challenge him, it is not surprising that his arrangements sound traditional and almost conservative today. Trying to explain his job, Hefti quotes Neil Simon, who told an interviewer: "I'm not a great writer: I'm a great listener!" Hefti says—perhaps too modestly—about his work with Basie: "Just listening to him was the only thing I had to do." But Hefti also had the skill to capture the sound he heard, and the acumen to adapt it to the public's taste.

Hefti's arrangements and compositions are typically bright and cheerful—they have a daylight sound, to take his words out of context. High-minded critics might object to the modesty of his goals. Parents may shudder when their children chant the theme from *Batman*, a tune as unforgettable as an aspirin commercial or a steady drip. But Hefti will have an honorable place in the history of American music, if only for helping to bring Bill Basie into the light where he belongs. Hefti would have us believe that he is merely a highly skilled listener. He is not, however, only a mimic. Like most important artists he has helped to create the tastes he satisfies, and his big band works are among the best created since the swing era.

MARIAN McPARTLAND

Citing the careers of Bix Beiderbecke, Louis Armstrong, Charlie Christian, Jimmy Blanton and Charlie Parker, critics often suggest that jazz is a young person's art, repeatedly revolutionized by men and women in their twenties who are generally doomed to repeat themselves later in their careers. "Jazz," says Wilfred Mellers in his intriguing but unreliable *Music in a New Found Land*, "is of its nature an art of youth and adolescence, and the jazzman's spontaneity is most 'maturely' realized when he is least inhibited . . . The exceptional artist who does develop—for instance Ellington—does so only by a partial rapprochement with techniques and attitudes that do not belong to jazz at all." If, according to this argument, we find in a jazz performance something that can be called mature (without quotation marks), it is likely to be a non-jazz element appropriated by an increasingly inhibited musician, perhaps desperate for something new. Not every jazz musician acquires inhibitions with learning, however, and the role of the merely intuitive musician seems likely to diminish in modern music. At the same time it is dangerous to limit what can be said to "belong to jazz." Mellers allows that there is a kind of jazz musician who "refines and renders subtler his art without radically changing it." Occasionally, he should admit, there is an artist—like pianist Marian McPartland—who absorbs ideas from all over the jazz world while managing to express more and more clearly her own musical personality. Even her friends seem almost startled at the new depth and range of Marian McPartland's piano playing. Composer Alec Wilder wrote: "Until recent years I was aware of and impressed by the playing of Marian McPartland. Then, for some years I was out of touch not only with her playing but with that of every other worthy jazz musician. I was probably so depressed by the omnipresence of rock and its bedfellows that I presumed nothing else existed. When I finally surfaced and heard Marian play, I was no longer impressed, I was bedazzled. Indeed, I was more than bedazzled, I was jealous. In three unplanned minutes she can, and consistently does, invent rhythms, harmonic sequences and melodic flights which would take me three weeks to achieve as a composer. And even then, not half as well. She plays with great fluency, style, verve, with forthrightness and, along with astounding flow and sweep, profound warmth and affection."

McPartland has managed to turn an apparent disadvantage—a childhood in England that provided no early training with jazz bands—into a real asset: the flexibility most listeners hear in her work. Recently she said on National Public Radio: "I never had a foundation. I was always searching and looking and listening to other people." For NPR she has taped a series of interviews and performances with such diverse pianists as Teddy Wilson, John Lewis, Tommy Flanagan, Bill Evans, Chick Corea and Joanne Brackeen. Typically a two-piano duet with one of these musicians will end with Marian exclaiming, "What a kick that was!" She says she has learned something from each of the performers—about choosing the right tempo from John Lewis, or a new way of turning the beat around from Bill Evans. She is consistently adventurous ("I'd rather be wrong than work something out beforehand") and even stubborn in her search for new ways to play: "I'm nothing if not persistent," she told me.

Marian McPartland *by Fred W. McDarrah*

I talked to Marian McPartland before a performance in Boston, in which she was to appear in a Dixieland session with ex-husband Jimmy McPartland, clarinetist Kenny Davern, Vic Dickenson and Roy Eldridge. She had already discussed with Davern what he was to wear that evening, grumbling "I don't know why I should be the only one dressed up just because I'm a female" without hiding the fact that she *likes* that cool, elegant image she projects on stage. She has short blonde hair, loosely curled, and a smile that lifts and lights her whole face. She can be intimidating— I've seen her turn almost 180 degrees to stare at a boorish couple who were talking loudly during one of her sets; without dropping a beat she smiled freezingly at them until they were quiet. McPartland's a slim, attractive woman, who should be pleased with her appearance, but when Chick Corea suggested that he would improvise a musical portrait of her, she insisted, "Don't put in my nose," adding after the music had stopped, "I'm not that nice. Somebody told me once I was very violent." While we talked, Marian sat struggling with an allergy, her hair protected by a scarf. In the background Jimmy McPartland puttered around genially, making us tea, blowing into his mouthpiece, and bragging about Marian more in the manner of a bearish big brother than an ex-husband: "She's so broad musically—she can play old Dixieland, two-beat, all the way up to the most modern. She explores everything, and she has her own style in each idiom. I can't make that scene—I get in one groove and forget it."

Marian was born in Windsor, England, in 1920, daughter of a middle-class couple with little interest in popular music. She was given piano lessons after she showed a precocious interest in the instrument, picking out tunes with two fingers. In her early teens, she learned jazz—her sister's boyfriend brought over some records that only the younger girl appreciated: "I inherited the records and the boyfriend too. Soon I was hearing Teddy Wilson and Art Tatum and the Benny Goodman groups and Meade Lux Lewis—everything that was on records. In England, the people who did listen to jazz were really rabid—I think that's true all over Europe. Every small town in England had its own 'rhythm club.' People would get together once a week and play records for each other and catch up on the latest. So I heard what most people in this country were hearing, except that I was never somebody who could run around and hang around backstage, like a lot of kids do. With my family background, it just never occurred to me to go and try to meet these people. I would see names like Fats Waller on the Palladium billboard, and I would think, 'Oh how great.' It never occurred to me that I could go to hear him, or try to meet him. I would be scared stiff.

"My family wasn't the least bit interested. They would have been more happy if I played classical piano. I didn't even study classical music to any great extent until I went to the Guildhall School of Music when I was about seventeen. That's when my family finally decided I didn't fit into any of the categories they wanted me to fit into, like being a nurse, or being a bank clerk, or something they considered respectable. I left Guildhall before I graduated; I was offered a job playing in a four-piano vaudeville act.

"I don't think I ever consciously made a decision to be a musician. I went out with the vaudeville act, and I wasn't really playing jazz. I was probably playing a kind of pop brand of jazz, but at least I was out there, playing theaters all over England. I joined the USO camp shows and went to France. That's where I met Jimmy. Then I *really* started to hear a lot of records. There were those V-Disks, special records put out for the G.I.'s. That's how I first heard Stan Kenton's band, for instance. I would meet musicians that were playing in the different bands, and I got to playing with them. Not until I came over here did I really feel that I was beginning to be a player. When I listen to some of the things I did then, I sound awful, corny as hell—corny ideas, lack of percussiveness. I first heard bebop at the house of Charles Delaunay, the French critic. I was floored. I couldn't understand what the pianist was doing, and I remember asking Delaunay if the piano part were written down. Now it sounds so easy. When I first heard Coltrane's *Giant Steps* I thought, 'Oh Jesus, I'll never learn this,' but I did. The more you learn, the more you can learn."

Marian McPartland came to the United States after the war, playing in a Dixieland group with her husband. Jimmy prodded his wife to start her own group, and in 1951 she was leading a trio at the Hickory House and the Embers in New York City. "When I started out, I had to get over the trauma of telling people what to do and what tunes to play. But I didn't feel inhibited because I was a woman. I might have if I hadn't been in the position of being able to hire people. I always hired the best guys there were. My first trio included Don Lamond and Eddie Safranski, then Joe Morello and Bill Crow. You can't do better than that, and everybody was very helpful. At the Embers, during the first gig I had, they hired Roy Eldridge and Coleman Hawkins. Eddie Heywood was working opposite us, and he didn't want to play for them. Needless to say, I was only too thrilled to be the one that got to play with them. I always considered that one of my great experiences. I've got the pictures at home to prove it. That was a kick.

"I think improvising came naturally to me. The quality of my improvising has changed, but I always could improvise, and I think just about everybody should be able to. From hearing myself on records and tapes, I've learned what not to do. Some musicians have helped. I once took a valuable lesson with Lennie Tristano. I said, 'I want to take a lesson with you and have you tell me what you think about my playing.' Which was disastrous, because he was very cutting. He said, 'Well, if you want to be a romantic kind of player, you just let the time fluctuate. One minute you're going fast, the next minute slow. I think your time should be improved. You should go home and practice with a metronome.' He picked apart my playing—he said I was too busy. I think he was right—I did that. That's still one of my faults. I always tell kids, 'When in doubt,

JAZZ LIVES

leave it out.' But I don't take my own advice. I play and play and fill every hole, and I keep telling myself, 'Take a breath, let a space go by.' So I stop and it seems like an hour goes by. But when I hear it on the record, it seems perfect. You don't have to play madly all the time. I've grown more analytical; as I listen to Lennie Tristano now, I think that sometimes his idea of time was a little monotonous.

"Then afterwards, John Mehegan made a funny remark to me. We were at the Hickory House, and he was the intermission pianist. He said, 'Marian, you know there's just not enough Bird in your playing.' So I took that to heart. I knew what he meant by that too—I didn't have those Charlie Parker configurations. I was probably playing pretty ideas, instead of getting more funky.

"Ballads are my best kick. I think I'm very good at them. I'll challenge anybody to a ballad, but on up-tempo tunes, I'd hate to get mixed up with Oscar Peterson. At times I feel like I'm always one step behind. As soon as I mastered bebop, everyone went on to something else. Now I've got to the point where I can play a free tune with the best of them. I'd challenge anybody to a free tune, including Cecil Taylor."

While McPartland herself has become more analytical, her playing has gained in depth and flexibility. She is capable of suggesting the soft harmonies and elusive emotions of Debussy, or of borrowing a stomping bass figure from Mary Lou Williams. On ballad performances, she might offer a spare, bare-bones version of the melody, drift a bit over some bass chords until, gradually adding flesh to the skeleton, she picks up the tempo and fills out the tune's harmonies, ending reflectively with a return to the original statement. Like many accomplished jazz musicians, she likes to tinge with blue an occasionally syrupy ballad, putting a little Bird in her playing with the crushed notes and strong 4/4 feeling of the blues. She is too critical of her up-tempo playing, which can be exhilarating—following a McPartland club date I once talked to an ecstatic Alec Wilder. He was overwhelmed not by the pianist's ballads but by the astonishing flow of ideas and technical facility of her up-tempo version of "I Got Rhythm."

McPartland still mentions the classical studies called the Hanon Exercises with awe and a little horror. She has not forgotten her classical training, and in recent years she has taken an unexpected step to justify her parents' expectations of her. "Last year I decided I would fulfill part of my teenage promise to my family, that I would study classical music. I suddenly had this urge to learn a piano concerto and to do some symphony dates. I learned the old war horse, the Grieg piano concerto. Everybody says, 'Why did you pick that one?' I say, 'I thought it was easy.' When I got into it I found out how wrong I was. I've performed it with the Rochester Philharmonic, with the Memphis and Chicago Civic Symphonies. I've got the Buffalo Philharmonic and the Minneapolis coming up. It's exciting, but it's a lot of work. Each time I play it I have to do all this woodshedding. I've started private studying again with a friend who teaches at the Manhattan School. Without her, I don't think I would have been able really to play the darn thing. I would have played the notes, but she helps with the interpretation and corrects my little idiosyncracies and the jazz things that creep in. Sometimes I don't play the thing the way it's written, and of course you have to with classical music. I do the Grieg in the first half of the concert and then I have to switch brains—in the second half I do some jazz things arranged for the symphony. I've got two of my own pieces arranged: 'Ambiance' and 'Willow Creek.' I do an arrangement of 'Eleanor Rigby' and a selection from 'West Side Story'—you wouldn't think people would still like to hear that but they do.

"I've mostly given up playing clubs. Recently I had a job at Michael's Pub [a club], but that was a labor of love. We were doing all Alec Wilder music, three weeks of his music with the singer Marlene Verplanck. We play half of the program, and she sings the other half. Wilder hasn't written too many popular tunes—after you've done 'I'll Be Around' and 'While You're Young' and 'It's So Peaceful In The Country,' where do you go? So Marlene dug up a lot of obscure Wilder songs. And I'll play 'It's So Peaceful' as a bossa nova, and then she'll come back the next set and sing it as a ballad. Some people don't even realize they're hearing the same tunes. Wilder has been glorying in it. He's there every night. He's always made a big point of being a recluse. He says he can't stand crowds and yet he'll go and sit in the front row.

"Alec tries to get me to compose more, but I haven't written anything lately. I've got a lot of half-written stuff on the piano. I should have some new tunes, because I'm beating the other ones to death. I can hardly find time to compose. I wish I had less to do. I work constantly at something—either performing or preparing to perform. Now I'm not taking any night-club dates because six nights a week really puts a crimp in your activities." Her attempt to wean herself of clubs is based also on the unattractive conditions in most clubs, with their smoke, dirt and noisy audiences. Despite this resolve, McPartland's schedule is so tight it's a wonder she can remember it. "After this concert, I've got five days off, then I'm doing two concerts back-to-back—one in West Virginia and then the Kansas City Festival. Then I've got about a week to practice the Grieg. I do it in Buffalo. Then the next day, I play with Teddy Wilson in Providence; then two more dates with him. Then I go to Schenectady for five days."

McPartland's NPR show certainly has demonstrated the range of her interest in pianists, an interest that extends well beyond the handful of musicians she was able to interview. "When I was beginning, I listened to Tatum, Jess Stacy, Teddy Wilson. Now of course I listen to Chick Corea, Keith Jarrett and Herbie Hancock, although I like the things they did years ago more than the recent things. I wanted to play Chick's composition 'Windows' on the radio show with him. He said, 'Let's see, how does that go?' and he couldn't get through it. I said, 'It's incredible you don't play that anymore—it's a beautiful tune.' We wound up doing

'Crystal Silence.' I still enjoy what Oscar Peterson does, although to me that is a follow-up to Art Tatum. I love the way Bill Evans has kind of stretched out and changed.

"I think if people don't change, it's a shame. I know some musicians who play exactly the same way now as they did twenty years ago. I really like to hear people grow, but not everybody does or wants to or can. What I'd really like to do myself is be a little more far out. I just seem to get stuck in a conservative situation. I think I will have to go and play some place like the Other End where the audience would be ready to accept things that are further out. Because I think I've built up an audience of fairly conservative types, who want to hear regular tunes."

She certainly is not conservative herself with her time or energy. Besides performing, McPartland is working on a book about the role of women in jazz, hoping to go as far back as Lil Armstrong. When the records she had made for Capitol, Savoy and other companies went out of print, she started her own label, Halcyon. The company has put out 13 records, most of them featuring McPartland's piano. She plays generous amounts of Alec Wilder, Gershwin and Cole Porter, and she also brings back such older standards as "New Orleans," which she turns into a slow blues. She ennobles some contemporary songs, especially ballads like Stevie Wonder's "You Are the Sunshine of My Life" or the often sentimentalized "Send in the Clowns." She floats her own impressionistic compositions, those with titles like "Ambiance," "Afterglow," "Glimpse," and the one most suggestive of her ensemble work, "A Delicate Balance." As she says, McPartland is most impressive on ballads, but she also has developed the percussive touch she needs for up-tempo tunes. Like Bill Evans, she has been able to nurture telepathic relationships with a series of bassists such as Brian Torff and Michael Moore. On one record she prods the latter into some delicate but expansive "free" playing. As she says, it's all a kick.

Once discouraged from music by her family, Mc-

Partland seconds the ambition of talented kids, going into schools from time to time to demonstrate improvisation. She also lectures parents on the subject of her profession: "I find as I talk to people that most parents don't want their kids to be musicians. That's the norm. They always think of the worst aspects of things: poverty, meeting undesirable people, bumming around. They think of all the terrible things. Well, I think musicians are a rare breed who are working at something they really like to do. You see so many people for whom the word 'work' conjures up something unpleasant, whereas for us, going to work means something pleasant. We can do it for money or if we choose to do it for no money, that's okay too. As far as I'm concerned, it was never work. It's usually fun. Why can't parents see that?" Marian McPartland should convince them if anyone can—she doesn't smoke or drink, she works hard, and she's normal in all the accepted ways. When she sits down at the piano she sparkles—even, I imagine, when she sits down to play Grieg.

SONNY ROLLINS

When Sonny Rollins returned to the American jazz scene in 1972 after the third of his self-imposed sabbaticals from public performance, he overwhelmed audiences once again with the sheer power and intelligence of his playing. His tone had broadened—it had a growling edge to it, and Rollins began using an almost raucous vibrato. His playing was confident, even exuberant. On a good night, he would open his set by wandering into the audience playing a long, unaccompanied solo, unamplified and uninterrupted. He would play a little rhythmic figure, then repeat and vary it, either developing a motif or dropping it to introduce a snatch of a popular song or a theme of Dvorak's. He moved from tune to tune: it was amusing to watch his band pick up their instruments at what seemed to be their cue, and then lower them again as Rollins entered a new area with his solo. He seemed restless, happy and totally in control, even of rude New York audiences. One night at the Village Gate I saw him face a noisy crowd. When a drunk approached him with a request in the middle of a solo, Rollins played a mocking phrase that accompanied the boor back to his seat. Disgruntled at an audience's reaction to a ballad, Rollins countered with a hard-bopping blues that made one realize why musicians refer to their horns as "axes." During the weeks at the Village Gate in 1972,

Rollins changed his rhythm section nightly; he was rediscovering his sound and was forced constantly to impose his ideas on a new group that was in awe of him. His audiences shared his joy at his ability to overcome all the musical obstacles he confronted. Typically his ballads ended with an extended, virtuosic cadenza, and he finished most sets with a long, floating rhapsodic solo on one of his bouncy calypsos. Known earlier for his use of silence and space, for his orderly improvising and for his often sardonic wit, Rollins in 1972 seemed ready to add an ecstatic lyricism to his other styles: he was singing in full-throated ease.

Considering the near mastery of music and environment that Rollins demonstrated at the Village Gate, one has to wonder about the three-year hiatus in public playing. In various interviews Rollins suggested that the reason for the most recent retirement had been his dissatisfaction with the music industry rather than with his own playing. Still, Rollins is, as Dexter Gordon has said in his most oracular tones, "a very complex man." Rollins's perplexing performance at the 1972 Newport Jazz Festival in New York suggests this complexity. After his triumphant engagement at the Village Gate, Rollins was to play before the excited and expectant crowd filling Carnegie Hall. In his forty-minute set he seemed distracted and shy. He wandered on and off the stage; he began a piece, stating the theme, and as the second chorus started, just at the point when he should begin improvising, he seemed to freeze—and he restated the theme. Few people who saw them could forget the gently imploring looks that Rollins's guitar player Masuo gave him when the guitarist had played fourteen or fifteen choruses of solo and was hoping to entice Rollins back to the microphone. I have seen this curious and disheartening process several times since the 1972 Carnegie Hall concert. In 1978 Rollins toured with a small group, adding his friend, trumpeter Donald Byrd, as an extra attraction. At a concert in Boston, Rollins played a promising first set only to withdraw when Byrd came on stage. The trumpeter was out of shape, and his huffings and puffings offered

Sonny Rollins *by Michael Ullman*

little compensation to an audience eager for more of Rollins's saxophone. His reticence suggests that, at times at least, public performance is a burden.

One can understand the difficulty of playing night after night in the Rollins manner. He is a most orderly improviser. In a famous essay on Rollins's performance of "Blue Seven," Gunther Schuller describes Rollins's thematic improvisation, a technique that makes a Rollins solo more than a string of unrelated ideas, but that also imposes an intellectual burden on the improviser. The entire Rollins solo on that piece is based on a short motif, and Schuller comments: "Such methods of musical procedure . . . are symptomatic of the growing concern by an increasing number of jazz musicians for a certain degree of intellectuality." Rollins has said that until he read Schuller's article, he did not realize consciously what he was doing while improvising. It is likely that at times the demands of such a procedure are simply too much for even a musician like Sonny Rollins. I heard him play erratically in Boston one night; again and again he repeated the outlines of a tune, and then hesitated, like a hunter balking at a hedge, unwilling to cross the barrier into improvisation. When called back by an audience happy just to be in his presence, Rollins played a version of his most attractive calypso tune, "St. Thomas," in a manner so wooden and square that there were few protests when he did not return for a third set.

If his relationship towards his music seems complicated, so does his view of his audiences. He spoke to Bob Blumenthal of *The Boston Phoenix* about performing in the Jazz Workshop: "The audiences at the Workshop have been beautiful, but I never view that response as warmth; I look at it as more of a challenge. I can never begin to expect that from an audience, having been in this business as long as I have. Even though they may mean it, 'Oh, gee, we're glad to see you' and that whole love thing, it's hard for me to accept it as that. I still feel that I have to produce; even more so. I feel funny about the standing ovations, because I know how fickle audiences can be. I'm never really impressed—I mean, okay, I'm glad, but I never let it really overwhelm me." During his second retirement, he used to practice on the Williamsburg Bridge in New York; part of the appeal of this activity was that he could play to people who were just wandering by, and who expected nothing from him. When his performances on the bridge made the news, Rollins stopped going—too many people who knew Sonny Rollins were coming by.

Since his return in 1972, Rollins has been traveling with a series of bands, and he has been recording for Milestone Records. The first album, entitled puckishly *Sonny Rollins' Next Album*, is perhaps the best of the series. It contains a new calypso, "The Everywhere Calypso," a hard-driving blues performance on "Keep Hold on Yourself," and a marvelous "Skylark" that features one of his solo cadenzas. The playing is rhythmically a little stiff, and in that respect is inferior to his live performances. *Horn Culture* is notable for Rollins's version of "God Bless the Child" and for his chattering, clucking solo on "Love Man." *The Cutting Edge* was recorded live at Montreux in 1974, and *Nuclear* and *The Way I Feel* show Rollins moving closer toward rock and playing with larger groups. *Don't Stop the Carnival* offers virtuosic solos on "Autumn Nocturne" and two sides with Donald Byrd, demonstrating the trumpeter's soporific and inhibiting effect on Rollins. *The Way I Feel* is Rollins's most disappointing album. Not that it is totally unattractive, but one feels that Rollins could have done so much more with the material. He is supported by a large group, but the arrangements are unimaginative and the beat is heavy throughout: this is dance music. The real problem is Rollins. He has written an attractive tune in "Island Lady," but he seems unwilling to improvise seriously on it. On the final chorus he squeaks and honks until the tune is faded out. After hearing *The Way I Feel*, saxophonist Phil Woods suggested that while Rollins could make a wonderful jazz-rock album, on this one he did not "break out."

The metaphor is instructive. When Rollins is playing at his best, he exposes himself more than almost any other musician—his most satisfying recordings have been with small groups, often without a piano, and many of his best live performances have been unaccompanied. He has talked about the added harmonic freedom of a group without a piano, but now he plays with a small rock-oriented band with a pianist, a guitarist, an electric bass, and a heavy-handed drummer. The beat goes on whether Rollins is playing or not. With his new rock-oriented material, Rollins has found a new, younger audience. *Easy Living*, with its mixtures of ballads and rock numbers, suggests what one is now likely to hear from Rollins in a nightclub. He is trying out new group sounds. He told Bob Blumenthal, "You could say I've experimented, and I like to experiment, but a lot of the things I've done are based on whom I'm playing with; different musicians create different responses. I get who's available—if I've got a gig, I have to get a band together—so to a degree I'm a prisoner of my band. Even though I might be the leader of the band, I find myself playing with *them* a lot of times." The Rollins most jazz fans want to hear is the confident musician who can walk out alone amongst the audience, playing involved, witty, consequential solos, or who can soar lyrically above the light calypso beat of his accompanists. Currently we have only snatches of that kind of playing. Wary of the occasional but inevitable disasters that occur when a musician takes such chances, Rollins has insulated himself from these trials. Jazz fans might find him a "prisoner" of his band to a larger extent than Rollins himself realizes. The man who some fans call "the walker" is tied to the stage: he now plays with an electric pick-up in his horn, and its cord keeps him away from the audience. Still, no one should stay away from a Rollins performance, for the moments when he does "break out" are like nothing else in jazz today.

BETTY CARTER

Singer Betty Carter has been popular with other black jazz musicians since she began performing. When she visited Copenhagen in the mid-60s, tenor saxophonist Ben Webster, a tough but sentimental man, met her at the airport. He was holding a bunch of drooping posies and there were tears in his eyes. Miles Davis has spoken admiringly of her singing, and he toured with her in 1958 and 1959. In 1961 Carter toured with Ray Charles, and she was asked to record with him for ABC-Paramount. *Ray Charles and Betty Carter* introduced her to a large audience that will remember her girlish, innocent and then petulant voice responding to Charles's insistent blandishments on "Baby, It's Cold Outside."

By the time she recorded that song, Betty Carter had been singing publicly for fifteen years. Born Lillie Mae Jones in 1930, Betty Carter is a stylish woman whose physique is so striking that, playing at the Apollo Theater, "I would be about eight bars into my tune before anyone realized I was singing." Redd Foxx is said to have observed her for six months before realizing she could sing. She appears in filmy dresses or modish turtlenecks. She has round piercing eyes, a large, mobile mouth, and wears a variety of kerchiefs, hats and capes. Carter grew up in Detroit at a crucial time in jazz history. As a youngster she heard Louis

Armstrong, Billie Holiday, Coleman Hawkins and Duke Ellington. But she was also exposed to the innovators. "That was the bebop era too, so all that music was confronting me. Detroit was still full of musicians that caught onto bebop early and supported it. The environment was very good for anyone who wanted to do something in music." She first sang with Miles Davis in 1946 or 1947: "I sat in with him in Detroit before he had even learned to play the trumpet—when his notes were really tit for tat. I had to have the experience of sitting in with Charlie Parker and those guys. When they came into town, I'd be the first one there standing in line—a real fan, but a musician too. Because music was growing on me—it was magnetizing me." It was not merely music that was growing on her, but bebop in particular—the newest thing in music, already earning a reputation both as a beautiful, difficult form and as a music tied to the drug culture.

Betty Carter got her first break when she won a 1946 amateur contest in Detroit: "When I came up, there were a lot of theaters across the country that had an amateur show night—the Apollo, the Paradise in Detroit, the Howard in Washington, the Royal in Baltimore and Philadelphia, and the Regal in Chicago—a lot of theaters for young kids to try out their wares. It was all about show business at that time; it was about getting on stage and doing an act. So you had the chance to try out what you could do early and get told one way or another. I just sang and played the piano—I sang 'The Man I Love.' " Carter had a modest musical training. But more important than the lessons she'd taken was the fact that she was "a natural as far as rhythm was concerned and staying in tune." She had—still has—little encouragement from her family: "My family right now does not know a thing about what I'm doing. They have no idea. They are just like some of the audience out there that don't know a thing about Betty Carter. I never put myself on them. I left in '51 and there was nobody here on the East Coast. I didn't have anything to offer them: I couldn't say 'Bring the whole

Betty Carter *by Deborah Feingold*

family to New York.' So we never got really close and I was never able to call them and brag about what I'm doing."

At sixteen, Betty Carter started traveling, picking up jobs in black bars and theaters in the midwest. Again, things seemed easier for an unknown in those days: "It's not like today, when the first thing the club owner asks you is 'Where's your record.' " Carter learned to "scat," the wordless vocalizing introduced by Louis Armstrong and popularized by Ella Fitzgerald. All the bebop singers scatted. "The field was open if you wanted to scat. If you were interested in bebop you had to have a knowledge of improvising and be quick and fast. Otherwise you would just be ordinary."

From 1948 to 1951 Carter toured with the Lionel Hampton band. She stayed because she wanted to learn more about the business, about music, and also because Lionel Hampton's wife liked her. Her relations with Hamp himself were stormy. Leading a band with such young beboppers as Charles Mingus, Fats Navarro and Benny Bailey, Hampton must have felt a little defensive. There's a broadcast recording of the Hampton band at this time. In the middle of "Jaybird," Hampton introduces our Betty Carter by her pseudonym, "Lorraine Carter," and she scats a chorus in the true modern style. Hampton played such bebop tunes as "Hothouse," but he was jealous of the success of Dizzy Gillespie's band—an orchestra that always seemed to be following or preceding the Hampton band in its national tours. Hamp teased his young scat vocalist: "He would do things like get on the bus and ask me a question like, 'Hey Gates, whose band you like the best, mine or Dizzy's?' And I'd say, 'Dizzy's.' "

Soon he was introducing the girl who wanted to be known as Lorraine Carter as "Betty Bebop." "The name itself was catchy. Nobody forgot it—even though I hated it. And bebop was the thing among black people at that time. Betty Bebop—the young kid scatting with Lionel Hampton." But the "young kid" was restive: she was wary of being identified so closely with the name "bebop," if not with the music, for bebop was associated in some people's minds with the heroin subculture. "I knew I was going to have trouble later. You know, you have foresight. Here's a word that everybody's talking about 'down with,' which has nothing really to do with the music. Out of that dope-crazy world came the most creative music." The name Betty Carter seems to be a compromise: she took the "Betty" from Ms. Bebop, and the "Carter" from her more elegant pseudonym, Lorraine Carter. She stuck out the Hampton engagement, supported by Mrs. Hampton, who saw her potential, and by such figures as Frank and Bob Schiffman, managers of the Apollo Theater. When he was angry with Carter, Hampton would try to keep her off the Apollo's stage, but the Schiffmans insisted on hearing her.

It was worth staying if only because alto sax-ophonist Bobby Plater was teaching the young singer more about music. "It wasn't Hamp's encouragement that kept me going. I used his two-and-a-half years to learn how to write." She also learned how to read music, how to transpose, and how to face an audience, building enough of a following that after leaving Hampton in 1951 she could get a six-month engage-ment at the Apollo Bar "right down the street from the Apollo Theater, 125th St. and 8th Avenue. . . At that point I really started getting my music together: my ideas about programming my performances so that it will be interesting to me and my musicians and the audience." Throughout the '50s, Carter worked various gigs out of New York, including a job with Redd Foxx in Philadelphia and a "camp show down South with Man Tan Moore, down through Mississippi, Georgia, Alabama—swinging bebop in little theaters across the tracks." (Mantan Moreland is best known as the bug-eyed black sidekick in various Charlie Chan movies.)

She was still playing mainly to black audiences, and suffering, she felt, from the "split between white and black music." If a black artist such as Lavern Baker made a commercial hit, it would be "covered" by a white imitator—as Georgie Gibbs covered Baker's "Tweedledee and Tweedledum." As Carter sees it, black audiences were more demanding than their white counterparts, insisting that black artists be themselves. "A style is you—you can imitate somebody else's style. But in that time we dared not imitate. It wasn't easy for us as black people to imitate other great stars and make it. It didn't settle with us. A second Sarah Vaughan would never have the respect of the black community. In the white world, they imitated each other. Stan Getz had a lot of tenor players sounding like him, while he sounded like Lester Young. There were all those girls like Anita O'Day, June Christy, Chris Connor—and they all made it. There were never two Sarah Vaughans, or two Billie Holidays, or two Ella Fitzgeralds. Even in our dancing acts, our shake dancing, our tap dancing acts, we all strived to be our own person. That was my whole background, my whole foundation."

Racially, things started to change in the music business with the Beatles, who along with other British rock groups publicized their debt to black music. While others have said that jazz took a back seat to rock in the '60s, Carter states that "when the Beatles came into existence black music was accepted across the board. It was like it gave permission to every white artist who wanted to do some black material or to approach the black world of music—it was the stamp of approval. Elvis Presley had done it, but he never announced it." The "stamp of approval" meant that more white musicians were seeing the commercial potential of earlier innovations by black musicians. Only later did the innovators themselves benefit from the resulting publicity.

Carter's compositions came straight out of her life. "I Can't Help It," recorded as early as 1958, articulates a theme that recurs in Carter's conversation: her need to be herself and to express herself no matter what the consequence. "Have you considered what it does to your soul/You sell it when you play some other's role." She says about composing that "when the feeling is strong that there is something I need to say musically the melody comes—it just seems to float into my head. . . 'Open the Door' was a tune that I thought of in my relationship with my husband and my kids. I was trying to get him to understand what I was all about, to get to understand me more—why I couldn't give up what I was doing to go for the money." Her husband tried unsuccessfully throughout the '60s to get her to sing commercially, arguing that she could resume her "style" after she had made a hit. "I was trying to get him to understand and he never even heard me. He probably hears me now." The song pleads "Open the door, dear, and perhaps you'll find/You've had me on your mind."

Carter is justly proud that she has not compromised herself. When in the late '60s no major company would record her effective but demanding style, she created her own Bet-Car Records. She often sings ballads at absurdly slow tempos, bending and rolling each note, using a lot of space and silence. "Spring," I heard her say, "has got me feeling like" —a long pause— "a horse" —another pause during which she opens her eyes wide and the audience laughs— "that never left the pole." A silly lyric becomes a good joke. She has a small high voice, but she likes to sweep down to its throatiest tones. On stage she dances idio- syncratically—her body twists with and accents the music. She is ebullient on up-tempo, scat tunes, and affecting on tender, personal lyrics. She is free with written melodies, but careful with words.

Her professional life has made motherhood difficult. Her sons are now teenagers, and their father has been gone from the family for much of the younger one's life. "The difficult part was the mother anxiety about what's happening at home with the kids while the mother's gone. But you got to do what you got to do, and if you're strong enough nothing's going to happen. It could, but that's the chance you got to take." Now she looks back contentedly. "You can't hardly ask any more out of life—to have been doing my own kind of singing. I never tried to do anything else. I was never on welfare. I never quit. I never stopped singing for any length of time." Carter received a standing ovation at Newport, after her first performance at the festival, and the 1979 Festival dedicated a night to Betty Carter and her friends. She also has performed at the Montreux Jazz Festival. Her audiences are expanding. Using her favorite metaphor, one might say that recently Betty Carter has been "floating." She feels free: "I'm more musical now than I have been in all my life. You see the freedom the audience gave me last night. If I do something that I know is really musical and I get this wide-out smile from those young kids, it just lets you know how free I can be. Then with that feeling of freedom you can float through your music and they just come running to you. Because jazz is spontaneous. It's a beautiful feeling."

HORACE SILVER

Just into his fifties, pianist Horace Ward Silver is a forceful player and an engaging man. He prides himself on remaining open to all kinds of music and accessible to many kinds of people. Like Duke Ellington, who dedicated suites to Africa and South America, Silver has been inspired by his travels and by his heredity: his compositions include "Senor Blues," "Tokyo Blues," "Cape Verde Blues," and the lesser known "Baghdad Blues." He has long hair and a gentle smile. When amused, he hunches his shoulders and laughs, rocking his head in an elfin manner peculiar to himself. On stage he holds his shoulders high, drops his head over the piano and pounds out the beat with one or both feet, working one area of the piano at a time with his hands close together. He habitually chews gum: at the end of a recent club performance, there was a neatly arranged line of used gum placed at the end of his piano bench, one piece for each set.

Born in Norwalk, Connecticut, Silver arrived in New York in 1950 when the jazz world was disconcertingly "cool." At least to some observers, jazz seemed to be splitting between a modern, sophisticated form with complex harmonies and delicate rhythms, and a more emotional type of music, primitive though swinging. Silver's music, like that of Art Blakey and Miles Davis in the mid-50s, managed to capitalize on some of the harmonic advances of his peers while stressing the beat and that "healing feeling," as one of his titles suggests. His music is funky and direct, but it is also carefully voiced, arranged and rehearsed.

I talked to Silver about his life as he ate a frugal breakfast in a motel room. When he turned thirty, he decided that he hadn't been taking care of his body and eliminated unhealthy foods. This noon he was eating two peanut butter sandwiches, a pile of nuts, a banana, and several vitamin pills washed down with Sanka and honey.

Silver's father came to this country from the Cape Verde Islands, arriving at the fishing town of New Bedford with the proper papers, having worked his way over on the boat. Not a professional musician, the father was nevertheless steeped in the folk music of his culture: "He loved to play music: he plays guitar, a little violin, all by ear and all Cape Verdean-Portuguese folk music, mostly in the minor key, very simple, not too many chord changes." The father played in a little string band with his two brothers. "When I was a kid my father and my uncles used to give house parties a lot of times. There wasn't very much in the way of entertainment in Norwalk, Connecticut, when I was born—there still isn't. People used to give house parties on a Saturday night, and invite friends. The women—my mother and some of my uncles' girlfriends—they would all prepare food. Somebody would bring a bottle of whiskey, someone wine. The party would be in the kitchen—we had a large kitchen—and the place would be packed with people dancing. My father and my uncles would play the music on the guitar, the violin and the mandolin. It's different from the authentic Portuguese music from Portugal—but I suppose it's derivative of that. I remember as a kid when they would have some of those parties, I would have on those pajamas that your feet go into, that cover you all up. They'd let me stay up till the party started and then they'd put me to bed. I'd go to sleep, but then they'd be laughing and talking and dancing and I'd wake up in the middle of the night. I'd hear the music

Horace Silver *by Robert Parent*

and I'd get out of bed and go down the steps and sit on the edge of the steps and peek around and listen to the music and watch them dance. Somebody would see me—you know how they fuss over little kids. Somebody would bring me over something to eat, some potato salad or chicken or something, and let me stay a while. I remember it."

Later, Silver liked the feeling but not the naivete of his father's folk tunes. He composed two tributes to that music: "Cape Verde Blues" and "Song for My Father." "My dad through the years had always said to me, 'Why don't you take some of this Portuguese folk music and put it into jazz?' I never could see it. To me it always seemed corny—because I was born here into American music, whether it be jazz or whatever. But there is a feeling, something there that's valid. I didn't really get in tune with that feeling until I was invited by Sergio Mendes to his house in Rio de Janeiro. I went to see Carnival and went around to different places he was playing and sat in, and I was fascinated by the musical capabilities of some of the young musicians. They were all into bossa nova, which as you know was greatly inspired by our American jazz. I got turned on to that beat. So I got back to New York and I said, 'I'll try to write a tune using that rhythm.' I started fooling around and I came up with a melody and I realized it was akin to Cape Verdean—like something my dad would play. That was 'Song for My Father.' My father was very pleased that I did it. I put his picture on the cover of the album. After that I did the 'Cape Verde Blues.' He still would like me to take one of those authentic Portuguese-Cape Verdean folk songs and play it basically the same way they play. But I don't hear that."

Silver first heard jazz recordings sometime after he started taking piano lessons. "My first introduction to jazz was boogie-woogie. Back in the days when boogie was prevalent, Tommy Dorsey had a tune called 'Boogie-Woogie'—it was Pinetop Smith's tune. Dorsey had an arrangement which I copied off the records and played by ear. Then Earl Fatha Hines had a 'Boogie-

Woogie on the St. Louis Blues'—I copied that off the record by ear. Eddie Heywood had a boogie-woogie arrangement on 'Begin the Beguine'—I copied that off the record by ear. I copied some Jay McShann off the records. I was about twelve. I used to be the hit at the little teenage parties." The youngster learned that although it was harmonically simple, boogie-woogie was not simple to execute—it took "a good strong left hand."

Silver also listened to recorded folk blues. "I liked and still do like all them old down home blues singers like Muddy Waters, Lightning Hopkins, Peetie Wheatstraw (the devil's son-in-law), Memphis Minnie. I dig the feeling. They weren't technicians but they had a whole lot of feeling. It was diamonds in the rough, unpolished diamonds." Curiously, even today Silver is known for his strong left hand and for the earthy, bluesy feeling his music projects. Some critics, however, find his ballads less convincing. During his first session for Blue Note in 1952, Silver recorded three originals and "Thou Swell." After some pounding introductory chords, Silver states the Richard Rodgers melody casually between repeated, resonant left jabs: the performance is powerful but not pretty.

Silver learned to play standard melodies only after he had captured the boogie-woogie rhythm and the feeling of the blues. "It wasn't until later that I could play tunes. I could improvise in my head. I used to walk down the street singing or whistling improvisations on 'Body and Soul' or some other standard tune and be so drugged that I couldn't find it on the piano." The young musician received some help from older players in the neighborhood and he bought Frank Skinner's book on harmony.

As he was exposed to new influences, he always hoped to apply what he learned to his own playing. "I started digging Tatum and Teddy Wilson. Of course Tatum was too fast for me—I couldn't copy him. Very few can. I could just sit in awe of what he did. I bought a Tatum piano folio once, and I never could play it. It was like someone took some ink and just splattered it all over the page. Then I bought a Teddy Wilson folio and I could play some of that. I could take a little of what Teddy Wilson did off the record, some of his simpler things . . . Then came bebop. I heard Charlie Parker and Dizzy Gillespie. It sounded weird to me at first. I couldn't get with it because it was so different. After listening a few times over and over, it started to sink in and I started really to like it. And then I heard Bud [Powell] and was fascinated by Bud and Monk. When I heard Monk it sounded weird to me too. In fact I thought Monk was putting everybody on. It's just that he was so unique, so radically different that you can't get into him right away. After listening to him for a while, I finally realized that the man is sincere and that's just really the way he plays. I love Monk's writing—his harmonies are so unique, it's beautiful."

By 1950, at twenty-two, Silver was playing the Sundown Club in Hartford with Harold Holdt, a swing saxophone player. They played for dancing and floor shows, and they also got to stretch out. Stan Getz played a one-nighter with Holdt's group, then hired the whole rhythm section. Soon Silver was living in New York, and playing with such musicians as Terry Gibbs, Miles Davis, Stan Getz, Art Blakey, Lester Young and Coleman Hawkins. He found some support from the manager of Birdland: "I almost became a house piano player at Birdland for a time. I used to go down there to practice during the day because I didn't have a piano. The manager liked me, so when some of the second groups were put together, they'd throw me in there. So I might be there one week with Slim Gailliard and then a couple weeks later with Chubby Jackson, Bill Harris and Serge Chaloff."

Silver remembers the five or six months with Lester Young as "one of the most beautiful experiences of my musical career." He found Prez "a very easy-going guy," although an introvert. "If you were a member of his band and he opened up to you, he was beautiful. He'd keep you laughing all the time." Still Silver recognized that Lester Young was a haunted man who hid from audiences and who at times used his now-famous slang to insulate himself. Silver remembers a time in Detroit when Lester Young ordered a sandwich and coffee in a diner, and Silver had to translate before the waiter could understand. "Prez'd feel like nobody liked him. But I could understand that because he went through hell being an innovator. He had the nerve to be daringly different, so everybody was putting him down—critics criticizing his tone, criticizing his playing—some musicians too. It scarred him inside.

"I was riding home from a gig one night in the car and I don't know how we got into this conversation, but somehow I felt he felt dejected or something and he told me—he called everybody 'Prez'—he said, 'Well, Prez, I really don't think nobody really likes old Prez.' I said, 'Well, Prez, how can you say that? You've got all of those tenor players idolizing you and trying to play like you—from Stan Getz to Zoot Sims to Al Cohn to Dexter Gordon and Gene Ammons.' He said, 'Yeah, but I don't know, Prez. I just don't feel like nobody really likes old Prez.' That's the way he felt. He was a very sociable person if you could get next to him, but he'd come off the bandstand and go right in the dressing room. He wouldn't go out till it was time to go on the bandstand again. If we were on the road he'd stay in his hotel room all day, and he'd either send out for food or get his food in a paper bag and come back and eat it in his room."

Coleman Hawkins Silver found "more outgoing than Prez. Prez was more of a pretty player. Hawkins had more of a hard-driving, bashing kind of swing," the kind Silver associates with Art Blakey. "Playing with Art Blakey, you'd have to play a more propulsive, hard-driving beat . . . Art is native-like—it's like going into the jungle."

Silver played with several Blakey organizations; each dissolved when the black musicians were unable to find work. "The first band I played with Art—a nine-piece band consisting of three saxophones, trumpet, trombone, piano, bass, drums and conga drum—could hardly get arrested. A good band, but we could hardly get a gig. We played for dances mostly; when those black clubs, the Elks or somebody, would give an affair, we'd play for their dancing. Ray Copeland wrote most of the arrangements—a lot were reminiscent of Tadd Dameron." The next Blakey group Silver played with was the famous band that included Clifford Brown. The band made two records for Blue Note, both still in print, but it only "lasted for a few weeks, because there was no place to play." Besides the scarcity of clubs, the band had to contend with racism: relatively unknown groups of white players could find work while the Blakey group sat at home. Back with Blakey a third time, Silver became a member of an informal corporation, the original Jazz Messengers. The band members, Kenny Dorham, Hank Mobley, Doug Watkins, Silver and Blakey, split evenly what money they earned and shared the business duties. "Musically it worked out great, but not in terms of the corporation." The musicians were not equally responsible about business, and the failure of the group convinced Silver of the need for a strong leader.

In 1954 Silver played and recorded with Miles Davis. For a while Silver and Davis lived in the same hotel on 25th Street. "I had a little upright piano in my room and Miles used to come in all the time and play it. I learned a lot of things from him about music. He's a hell of a teacher." Silver remembers Miles playing some of his ideas for the famous "Walking" session. He also remembers that Miles did not own a trumpet at the time—he had to borrow one for the session.

That same year Silver recorded some of his most popular compositions: a jaunty tune called "The Preacher," and the humorous, funky "Doodlin." In 1956 came "Senor Blues," the Latin-influenced 12-bar blues that helped make him a leader. "I started my own group quite by accident. After I left the Jazz Messengers, I thought I would cool it for a couple of months and do some practicing and lay back. While I was doing this, I got a call from my agent in New York [Jack Whittemore]. He said, 'There's a club owner down in Philadelphia at the Showboat who wants you to come in there with a band.' I said, 'Well, I ain't got no band. I

ain't no bandleader. I don't want that responsibility.' "
But Silver put together his first group. He has been a
leader ever since.

He was reassured about his potential both by
experience and by a stranger source, a numerologist in
California who told him he was destined to lead. He has
absorbed the mystical theory in his drive toward
perfection: "The most difficult thing in life is the most
important thing, perfecting one's self, one's
character," Silver says. Numerology has helped him
identify his "negative traits." His name, for instance,
lacks the numbers 2 and 7 and therefore his character
lacks the virtues of those numbers: hence the title of
one of his recent compositions, "In Pursuit of the 27th
Man." In fact the development of Silver's philosophy
can be charted by the evolution of his titles: from
"Filthy McNasty" to "I Expect Positive Results."
Silver's belief in the power of positive thinking is at
least partially a response to the rigors of the music
business, a business that scarred Lester Young and
embittered Roland Kirk. Silver notes: "I've been ripped
off in my earlier life, my compositions, and I used to be
bitter about it. I don't feel that way anymore. What's
past is past and I can't hold grudges. The fault is in you
if you can't handle a situation right. Duke Ellington
said it in an interview one time on TV. The interviewer
asked, 'Mr. Ellington, we hear you've been ripped off a
lot through your career—they've stolen your compositions or haven't paid you. Are you bitter about
this?' He said, 'Oh, no, I can't afford to be, because I'd
only be hurting myself.' And that's true. He took the
positive viewpoint."

A successful bandleader for over twenty years, one of
the most important composers in modern jazz and one
of the music's most effective accompanists, Silver now
lives in California. He works clubs and concerts from
June to September, and then goes to New York to record
for Blue Note, the same company that he has been with
for twenty-five years. Recently he has been investigating the elements of his heredity. *Silver 'n'
Percussion* contains two suites, one dedicated to Africa

and the other to the American Indian. "My family was very racially mixed—we had white, black, Portuguese and Indian—my grandmother's mother was a full-blooded Indian." The album took seven weeks to complete—longer than the life of several of his groups in the old days. He is now studying the music of James P. Johnson. He is also working on improving himself: after being silver for fifty years, he said, "I'm going to be gold."

DEXTER GORDON

Dexter Gordon is a tall, handsome, confident man with a cavernous baritone voice that he uses sparingly, and a boyish grin that is as disarming as his general demeanor is imposing. A sober looking six-foot-five, with hair graying gracefully at the temples, Gordon moves slowly and speaks deliberately. In 1976 he returned to the American club scene after living for a decade in Copenhagen, and he was immediately able to present his music to large crowds and an excited press. Hailed as a patriarch of bop who had mastered the later innovations of John Coltrane and Sonny Rollins, the tenor saxophonist was recorded almost immediately by CBS. In 1978, Gordon was voted *down beat*'s Jazzman of the Year.

Gordon is generally credited as being the first tenor player to incorporate adequately the styles of Charlie Parker, Dizzy Gillespie and Thelonious Monk. Since his tone was less expansive than that of Coleman Hawkins and his rhythm more insistent than that of Lester Young, Gordon was able to use the new harmonic sense and intricate rhythms of bebop, forging a powerful style of his own. Where Lester Young might linger (and in later years languish) behind the beat in a tantalizing fashion, and where Charlie Parker would display his virtuosity in tense ripples of sound, Dexter Gordon will solo with a heavy, aggressive but flexible beat, rocking with a steady roll, as the blues lyric puts it. While he is an emotional player whose up-tempo blues performances are intense and exciting, he is never hysterical—he maintains a level of detachment that allows him to quote "Here Comes the Bride" in the middle of an otherwise strikingly committed chorus. Gordon uses the whole range of his instrument: he can shriek in the top range that Coltrane discovered or honk at the bottom à la Illinois Jacquet. He roams fluently through a spacious ballad, and can modulate his tone from a wide, warm vibrato to the hard tight sound appropriate to up-tempo pieces. In the '40s Gordon was enthralled by Lester Young, whose music "told a story." Now, before playing a ballad, Gordon will ensure that his audience gets the story by intoning its lyrics impassively, grinning afterwards at the impression made by his sober delivery of the often inane lines ("Suddenly it seemed like polka dots and moonbeams,/All around a pug-nosed dream"). He shows that he is aware of lyrics in more subtle ways too: in a solo on the Billie Holiday hit, "You've Changed," I heard Gordon quote "I'll Never Be the Same," which he followed with "As Time Goes By," creating his own story of failed love. Charismatic and witty, Gordon has nonetheless made his greatest impact on audiences through the sheer power of his playing. Not surprisingly, some of his most satisfying creations over the years have been tenor saxophone battles, where two musicians alternate solos and trade phrases in a form that can resemble a polite parlor game or a gruesome downhome rumble.

Before emerging as a bebop star, Gordon was apprenticed in Lionel Hampton's band for three years, where he was second tenor behind Illinois Jacquet (who taught him how to honk); for three weeks he was in a Fletcher Henderson congregation (which must have taught him how not to run a band); and finally for a short time in 1944 he played in the Louis Armstrong big band. There is a bootleg recording of this band on which Armstrong sings a chorus of "Ain't Misbehavin'" and then announces archly, "Brother Dexter."

Gordon obliges with a solo that is rhythmically stiff and that contains audible signs of Jacquet's influence. Playing with bands not necessarily congenial to his style, Gordon welcomed the discipline required of a member of a reed section. The Dexter Gordon who recorded in 1945 with Billy Eckstine's big band is completely in control. His solo on Mr. B's "Lonesome Lover Blues" is supple and fluent, with several odd harmonic twists near the beginning that add tension to an elegant performance. Also in 1945, he began recording regularly as a leader for Savoy Records. He was twenty-two years old.

Gordon's father was a Los Angeles doctor and a jazz fan whose patients included Duke Ellington and Lionel Hampton. He bought his son a clarinet and saw to it that Dexter studied harmony. Dr. Gordon took Dexter to the Los Angeles theaters to hear the most famous of the big bands, including those of Lunceford and Louis Armstrong. "All the bands played the theaters then. There was a band, a movie, some acts and singers." Gordon was exposed to the excitement of live swing music and he also bought records, amassing, he says, a sizable collection while in his early teens. Critics have noted the influence of Lester Young on Gordon's early playing; the saxophonist himself mentions lesser-known figures as well, musicians from his neighborhood and others that he heard on record. "I used to listen to the Woodman band in Los Angeles. It was a family band, led by the father. All the Woodmans were fantastic. Britt [a trombonist later to play with Charles Mingus, Duke Ellington and others] had a brother named Coney—I guess that was short for Cornelius. Coney was a piano player. Another Woodman was a very good tenor player known as Brother Woodman. Brother Woodman played tenor like Chu Berry. In fact he was about the only cat I ever heard that could follow Chu's patterns. There were a lot of guys in those days who could play and I learned from all those guys.

"There was a tenor player with Andy Kirk named

Dick Wilson. He was something like Lester and Chu. He had a nice sound. He was with the Kirk band that had Mary Lou Williams. She was the first arranger I know of to write a tenor lead in the saxophones, so I listened carefully to her. The Kirk band had a singer—Pha Terrell. And they had a lot of hits, such as 'Until the Real Thing Comes Along,' which had a tenor lead and Pha Terrell singing. I didn't hear Kirk live until 1943. It was at the Orpheum Theater. They had three tenor players: Jimmy Forrest, J. B. King, and John Harrington. They had a couple of tunes that featured the three tenors too. The trumpet section was Howard McGhee, who was the soloist, and Fats Navarro, who had just come into the band. That was the first time I heard Fats. The theater had the band, a vocalist and a dancer. Somebody was dancing when I walked in, and there was an accompaniment to the dancer. Fats was playing just in the background. He made me stand right up and listen. The next time I met him was when he came into the Eckstine band, taking Dizzy Gillespie's chair. Fats used to tell me that while he was working with Andy Kirk, Howard McGhee was the featured soloist. Still, Maggie would let Fats take an occasional solo. He would solo and whatever note he would end on, that's the note Maggie would begin with. Fats would say, 'Man! That used to kill me!' "

As a youngster, Gordon benefited from the musical activity in the black neighborhoods of Los Angeles, playing in school bands, studying with important musicians, and associating with contemporaries who would soon be professionals. "There was a very strong musical thing in my neighborhood and we had some very good teachers. I went to Jefferson High School with people like Chico Hamilton, Melba Liston, Ernie Royal, Vi Redd. In another neighborhood there was a school with Charles Mingus, the Woodmans, Buddy Collette and others. In high school we had a very good teacher named Sam Brown—very dedicated. He had all these wild young dudes. We used to call him Count Brown. We had a school marching band, an orchestra that used to play light classics, plus a swing band that played stock arrangements of Benny Goodman and Basie hits.

"I studied with Lloyd Reese. At that time he was playing lead trumpet with Les Hite's band. He taught Mingus too. Reese formed a rehearsal band. Every Sunday morning we used to go down to the union building and rehearse. And different people—professionals—would write charts for us to practice. Nat Cole wrote a couple for us. He was one of the local piano players at the time. So I got a foundation in music in Los Angeles. I studied harmony and theory for two or three years. Studying with Lloyd Reese was important. He taught more than exercises in the books. He gave us a broader picture and an appreciation of music. He made us more aware. He was teaching us musical philosophy." When I asked Gordon what Reese's philosophy was, he looked surprised and responded, "Why, to play pretty."

While learning to play pretty, Gordon was working with a local group of youngsters who called themselves the Harlem Collegians. When he was seventeen, he joined the prestigious Lionel Hampton big band; it was soon after Hampton had left Benny Goodman. "The band was nearly formed and they had been rehearsing in Los Angeles for a couple of months and just before they were getting ready to leave one of the tenor players decided he didn't want to make the trip. So Marshall Royal, who was playing lead alto in the band, called me. He and his brother Ernie were both in the band, and Ernie and I had been in school orchestra together. I only had three days to get ready, which I'm sure is one of the reasons I got the call. There wasn't time to get someone of professional quality. We rode the bus from Los Angeles to Fort Worth, which took about seven days. We played the first night without a rehearsal. I didn't play a right note all night. Nobody said anything. The next couple of days we rehearsed, so I got a chance to become acquainted. I was really out of my league. I was with the band for three years. Obviously it influenced me. That was like going to college for me."

It was when he was with Hampton that Gordon first heard Charlie Parker, then with the Jay McShann band. Gordon's knowledge of harmony enabled him almost immediately to understand what Lester Young and now Parker were doing. As he told *down beat* interviewer Chuck Berg: "In the '30s cats were playing harmonically, basically straight tonic chords and seventh chords. He was playing the sixth and the ninth. He stretched it a little by using the same color tones used by Debussy and Ravel, those real soft tones. Lester was doing all that. Then Bird extended that to elevenths and thirteenths, like Diz, and to altered notes like the flatted fifth and flatted ninth. I was already in that direction, so when I heard Bird it was just a natural evolution. Fortunately, I worked with him and we used to hang out together and jam together in New York."

Some of Gordon's jam sessions have become legendary. A Los Angeles session of 1947 produced "The Hunt," a long performance that ends with the tenor saxophone battle of Wardell Gray and Gordon. Gray and Gordon, two tall, handsome players, one forceful and direct, and the other with more of the soft-toned Lester Young approach, should have become a commercially successful group. Gordon is puzzled that they did not: "Somehow my thing with Wardell was never exploited—at least in the positive way. There was nobody to promote it. We did things together, but it would just be a different club every night. We talked about traveling together, but in those days there were few managers or promoters around who might be interested. Most of the people in the business were gangsters. And also our personal lives were pretty chaotic—we weren't the most stable people in the world." Both Gordon and Gray were heroin addicts: in 1955 Gray was found dead in the desert outside Las Vegas, the victim of an apparent overdose, foul play, or both.

Gordon recorded only four times in the '50s, and his

career did not right itself until he signed a contract with Blue Note Records in 1961. His Blue Note recordings are consistently successful, demonstrating Gordon's ability to absorb something of the styles of Rollins and Coltrane. In 1963 Gordon recorded a session with another bebop legend, Bud Powell, a man nearly incapacitated by mental illness. Gordon elicited one of the best performances of Powell's later career: "I was living in Copenhagen at the time and Bud was in Paris. But he wasn't originally meant for the date: Kenny Drew was supposed to be the pianist. Kenny Drew was indisposed, so we got Bud. I had some music that I had written and that I planned on doing. We rehearsed for a couple of days—it was a catastrophe because Bud couldn't concentrate. He couldn't learn something new. So I told Frank Wilcox, 'I don't think we can do this.' He said, 'Let's go to the studio tomorrow and see what happens.' So I decided that the only way we could do the date was to bring in things we already knew. We did the standards—'Night in Tunisia,' 'Scrapple From the Apple.' There wasn't any pressure then on Bud. They came out perfectly—classic. But Bud had sort of stopped mentally. He was living and playing off his instincts and style. Every once in a while you could talk to him, and there would be some lucidity. Otherwise he was difficult to relate to, as he was still heavily medicated."

Gordon moved to Copenhagen in 1962. He found a congenial club, the Montmartre, and enjoyed the more relaxed atmosphere of Europe. He also enjoyed European audiences' respect for jazz musicians. Gordon bought a house, remarried, and fathered a son, returning periodically to this country to visit his mother and daughters in Los Angeles. After his extraordinary New York success in 1976, Gordon moved back to the United States. His first CBS recording was taped live at the Village Vanguard. Gordon commented on the date: "There was so much love and elation. Sometimes it was a little eerie at the Vanguard. After the last set they'd turn on the lights and nobody would move." Playing now as well as he ever has, Gordon is optimistic about the future. He is a strong man, with grace and style. "As you mature," he told me, "as you grow old, as you learn, you add something and take something out, but you're still yourself. I was always Dexter, Monk was always Monk. Can you imagine Bird not sounding like Bird? You don't just go out one day and pick up a style off a tree—it's inside." Gordon's press releases come today stamped "Bebop is the music of the future," and Gordon has become almost a symbol of the revival of what they call "straight-ahead jazz." He's modest enough to be surprised.

MAXINE GREGG

Though only in her late thirties, Maxine Gregg has been managing jazz artists for almost a decade. She runs MsManagement, an organization started by a group of women who wanted to use their various skills in a cooperatively run business. Gregg is the only survivor of the original group, but her business has thrived. A short woman who keeps herself well in the background, she is married to trumpeter Woody Shaw. She directs his career as well as those of Dexter Gordon and Johnny Griffin. All have had recent popular successes. Dexter Gordon was *down beat*'s 1978 Jazz-man of the Year, and Shaw's *Rosewood* was the favorite album of *down beat* readers in 1977. Many jazz fans will remember the triumphal "homecoming" of Dexter Gordon in 1976, when he was found newsworthy in this country for the first time in fifteen years. His return from Copenhagen, his home since 1962, inspired a new generation of listeners. If Dexter's 1976 homecoming was news, it was not because he was playing differently. Neither was it because he hadn't come home before: Gordon has family in Los Angeles and had been returning annually to see them, playing there, in Chicago, and often in New York City on the way. Gordon has attributed his recent success to fate, to the stars, to his being ready to play while rock musicians were degenerating, to timing. When I talked to Gordon, he mentioned MsManagement.

Maxine Gregg has worked as an agent, a road manager and a news promotor of jazz events. A dynamic, optimistic woman, she has a unique position from which to view jazz life. The office, which she shares with record producer Michael Cuscuna, is a barely converted apartment, with three desks in a living room whose walls are covered with pictures of Shaw and Gordon, as well as a shot of Maxine Gregg sitting on the White House lawn close to Jimmy Carter. An important person in jazz management, a "field of people who could fit into this room," she attended the President's party honoring jazz and its creators. As we talked Maxine's baby, another Woody Shaw, lay on the floor between us.

"I started doing this work full-time about seven years ago. The reason I got into it was that nobody was doing it. There was a real need, but I started as a fan. I started going to hear jazz very young. I was fifteen— I'm thirty-seven now. When I was in my early twenties and I used to go to clubs, Kenny Dorham or someone— one of my friends—would look out for me. He would tell the guys, 'Don't mess with her.' Because it's hard sometimes for a woman even to be a fan. Anyway, I was a fan who got pulled into the business. I was a freelance editor for technical books for a long time. I had been in the political movement. I always worked. I read some books, and musicians started coming up to me and I would show them how to set up a publishing company or how to do their copyright forms. I did grants for them for the National Endowment. They came to me because I was around the music, and because I was an editor.

"I first started managing when my friend tenor saxophonist Harold Vick came to me. He was in a group with Jack deJohnette called Compost. They were on Columbia Records, but they had no representation at all and they were floundering around. They had a record deal, but they couldn't get a manager. I saw the problem with Compost: they really couldn't do it themselves, and nobody would help them." Gregg

Maxine Gregg *by Deborah Feingold*

notes that it's quite possible for a musician to have a recording contract with a major label and still be unable to find work. Not every artist is actually promoted by the record company he signs with.

Gregg couldn't save Compost, but soon she was acting as road manager for the Gil Evans big band. It was a trying life: "The road manager does whatever you have to do to make sure that the band gets to the gig. You make the travel and hotel arrangements. When you have a big band, you can imagine getting them all in a plane. You get the tickets, you get them to the airport, you get them to the hotel, you get them to the gig, and you make sure they start on time. You collect the money. You pay them. The next day you do it all again, except you might need three cars. You make sure the sound system is balanced. Plus there's always a crisis. I went to Europe where I worked for a Dutch agent as a road manager. One of the reasons the business is going well now is that I spent those years traveling with road bands. I understand what that's like—and it's hard. What musicians go through before they stand up and play is unbelievable. I would be a wreck. In 1974 I managed Shirley Scott, who was trying to get some stuff together. Then Harold Vick had a heart attack. That was when we put on a benefit for him which made a lot of money. That was one of the first things I organized and promoted. McCoy Tyner played, and Dizzy Gillespie. I think it was at that point that I decided that I had better do this full-time. When Harold got sick, I said, 'People need help.'

"MsManagement was my idea. There were four other women involved—all women who were working free-lance and had different skills. One woman was a photographer-journalist who had been laid off by *Life* magazine, another friend had been an art director, and I had a friend who was in the political movement who talked very well—I thought she would make a good agent. The last woman just wanted some career. The idea was that if you can see clearly what you are good at, you can always work. I don't like to work for anybody, so I had to have my own business. I believe that if you can get help from people who are like-minded, you can get something going. We did other projects—we organized the opening of a campground in Jamaica called Strawberry Fields; I wasn't crazy about the name. In return we were allowed to go there for free. I still go."

Gregg met Dexter Gordon while working for a booking agent in Europe. "Dexter was traveling as a single in different countries and picking up different rhythm sections. There were some problems, so the agent flew me over to travel with him. I had only heard him on records. I walked into a club in Nancy, and I heard him and said, 'Wait a minute, this guy is fantastic. We don't have anything like this at home.' Ben Webster was in Europe, Lucky Thompson wasn't playing, Trane was dead, and Sonny Rollins was weird. There were no tenor players in that style. So I asked Dexter if he'd thought about coming back to the United States. He said, 'No, I heard that nothing was happening.' I said, 'You can make something happen.' Six months later he wrote to me and asked me if I would do something." Ms. Gregg adds, "The rest is history," with a mock-heroic grimace.

Gordon's return was carefully prearranged by Ms-Management. Gregg had to convince club owners, critics, and the public that Gordon was "current." Using one of her favorite words, Gregg said she had a "concept" for the tour. The concept was "homecoming." "The first gig I did with Dexter I did intentionally at Storyville [a small New York nightclub] for ridiculously low money so that the critics would come, so that it would be reviewed in the *Times*, and so that they could do stories on him in the *Voice*. You have to start the momentum. Timing had a lot to do with it but I worked on the tour for a year. I worked on advance publicity with the concept of homecoming. My first press release on Dexter went out and said that he would be back after, I think we said, seven years. We called it seven. Well, the truth was he had been coming back every year. But nobody knew it. He came to L.A. and Chicago and four years before he had been at the

Village Vanguard and nobody was there to hear him. But if you announce that he's coming back for the first time in seven years and he's the great Dexter Gordon, people will be there. It's as simple as that.

"I planned it very carefully. When I first made calls on Dexter, nobody wanted him. Max Gordon [owner of the Village Vanguard] didn't want to book him. They said he'd been away too long, that he wasn't interesting. Everybody's so caught up in the current stuff that they forgot. I knew that Bruce Lundvall [the president of CBS] had been a tenor player. When I worked for Compost, he was the vice president for marketing for CBS and we used to talk about jazz all the time. So I invited him and the people from the other record companies to the Vanguard and they all wanted to sign Dexter. There were lines going down the block the night he opened the Vanguard. Woody had put the band together for Dexter, which encouraged him to play on a certain level. Woody had played with Dexter in Europe and was one of his big boosters—he told *everybody* how great he sounded. You need to have the hard core following among the musicians and Woody made sure Dexter had that." When Dexter Gordon played a second engagement at the Vanguard, it was to record *Homecoming* for Columbia Records.

Gregg chose the Vanguard purposely: "A lot of people think Dexter and Woody are too big to work the Vanguard because it only holds 130 people. But the Village Vanguard is the oldest jazz club in the country, and people come to New York from all over the world to go to the Vanguard. You can get a South American tour because someone heard Dexter in the Village Vanguard. College students go there—it's a central place."

Gregg's experience with Compost demonstrated to her that for a musician a record or a job is not enough: a career depends on foresight. "Every gig has to be billed into the future. If you work in a club in Chicago and don't come out of it with five college dates for the next season, then I don't consider a week in Chicago successful." The recent success of Dexter Gordon and

Woody Shaw has depended on what they did in the past. Shaw, for instance, made his first recording on Eric Dolphy's *Iron Man* session in 1963. He was eighteen. Dolphy invited the teenager to join him in Paris, but died before Shaw got there. Shaw went to Europe anyway and then returned to the United States to play with such figures as Horace Silver and Art Blakey. He moved to San Francisco and worked as a single, gradually building a following and barely making a living. "All those years with all those gigs, Woody lived in San Francisco. He might be asked to go to Calgary, Alberta, as a single. Somebody there would have heard him with Silver. Dexter used to be the same way. They'd really want you to come, they send you a plane ticket, get you a hotel room, and give you a few hundred dollars. No real money, but if you're not doing anything and you don't have a band, that's good. When you think of all those years with that kind of gig, a lot of people must have heard him and remembered him. Also Woody built a big audience doing jazz clinics at schools. He and Joe Henderson did them for years in the summers. Hundreds of kids would come. They would play in places where they could never get a gig. The music publisher Jamie Aebersold put out a book of Woody Shaw's compositions and the book sold a lot. Jamie and I were shocked at how many trumpet students there must be."

Shaw recorded throughout the '60s and early '70s for smaller labels like Contemporary and Muse. Then in 1977, Columbia Records, alerted by Miles Davis, who said Shaw "has a lot of heart," bought Shaw out of his Muse contract. (Shaw wanted to be on Columbia because it was Davis's label.) The result of the new contract was that Shaw became a successful band leader; he was selling records. "Any Columbia record sells 10,000 copies," Gregg says, "which is good for a Muse or Bee Hive record. *Sophisticated Giant* [Gordon's second record for CBS] has sold over 75,000 copies. I estimate that [Woody Shaw's] *Stepping Stones* will be about 40 or 50,000. But I never say how many records an artist sells, I say how many records a company sells. The problem is to reach the people who don't know what jazz is. Woody's brother is on a football team, and his friends say to him, 'Woody Shaw's your brother?' Because they've heard the name, but they have no idea what he does, what kind of music it is. Woody told his brother, 'What do you mean, what is it? It's your music.'"

The usual strategy for expanding the jazz audience is to address rock fans. But Gregg thinks that classical music listeners are at least as likely to be converted. "If your ears have been burned out listening to rock and roll, you're not going to like jazz. Those listeners won't have the patience to appreciate Dexter Gordon. After all, there are people over thirty who buy records. Enough of this marketing for fourteen-to-eighteen-year-olds. That's a concept set up by people in their twenties who don't know any better. There are a lot of older fans who went away from the music at the time of the avant-garde and the Beatles. We lost a lot of people for straight-ahead music in the '60s. One reason Dexter Gordon is so successful is that he is a link—he influenced John Coltrane and was later influenced by Trane. He's as modern as anybody. Woody says Dexter is avant-garde. He can play 'out.' Woody doesn't even play his tune 'Moontrane' anymore because, he says, Dexter played so much on that tune that there's nothing else to play. And it's a very modern, difficult tune."

One aspect of Gregg's job today is to harass Columbia Records. MsManagement will call the record company three or four times a day. A company as large as Columbia has representatives all over the country, including in the major colleges. They have an artist development department, and they are capable of making a competent artist famous. But they also have many performers to deal with. Gregg's business is to see that the company is informed about her artists. A major record company is "a huge monster filled with people who don't know what to do. You can tell them. But it takes a lot of time to keep record companies informed. Musicians have to practice and to sleep. Few of them can manage their business too. We have to make the company aware of what the artist is doing. They have to know about every job. We want to know that they are in contact with the market, that they have records where Woody and Dexter are playing, that they promote the concert with advertisements, posters. The artist development department is supposed to get artists on national television, to assist in putting jazz in venues where it never appeared before. If I have a college date, I see that they notify the college reps, who can generate a lot of interest. I make sure that the people employed by Columbia in the field are aware of our artists. We try to get these people to hear Woody and Dexter—you can't sell something if you don't know what it is."

Many of the best jazz agents are women, says Gregg, speculating that this is because "the way we as women are socialized enables us to work although we don't get any credit. You wouldn't last if you do this work to get public recognition—that you'll never get. All day we're doing something for other people who are too busy to say thank you. We brought Johnny Griffin back to this country after fifteen years for a tour. We signed him with Fantasy Records, and then we read in the newspaper that a Chicago nightclub owner, Joe Segal, was given credit for bringing Griffin back. 'Okay, Joe,' I said, 'next time you pay for his plane ticket.'"

Gregg has had to deal with sexism. She remembers the picture she made when she was traveling as the road manager of jazz bands touring Europe: she would come into a hotel, a white woman traveling with five or six black musicians who were dragging cases and cases of luggage, instruments and so on. "It's not your average B flat," Junior Cook observed—not the usual thing.

At first she wasn't taken seriously as a businesswoman. Now, "all the agencies want to handle my artists." And her management has put such well-known artists as Gordon on a solid financial footing. For the first time in his life, in 1978 Gordon was able to keep a band on salary. Part of the struggle has been to get artists to take themselves seriously. "A lot of times jazz musicians don't even have the concept of needing a manager. They don't see the future in big terms. They just think of the next gig. They ask, 'Can you get me a gig?' I say, 'I don't even do that. That doesn't mean anything.' I asked Dexter once, 'When you and Wardell Gray had that band in 1947—that was one of the heaviest things I ever heard in my life. Nobody came to you and said, 'You can really do something with this?' It was commercial, it was hip. These were two musicians who sounded good and looked good. Dexter said no. It's something that is completely new, the idea of having a manager. Fortunately Dexter and Woody have long-range vision; some people just think about next month or next week."

Her ability to use her long-range vision is what makes Maxine Gregg "a very influential personality," as her husband told Robert Palmer, the current jazz critic at *The New York Times*. Because of her success, Gregg is often asked for advice. At times she feels it is presumptuous to give it: "Musicians—people with established names—often say to me when I ask them when they are going to make a record, 'Well, nobody asked me.' Well, nobody asked anybody. You either ask yourself, or put yourself in a position to be asked. You have to play somewhere, you have to be reviewed so that people will know you have a group. You have to do something first. But it's difficult for some people to know what to do first. They say, 'I'll get a group together when I have a gig.' Well, how are you going to get a gig when you don't have a group? And if the group isn't rehearsed and you get a job, it's going to sound bad. There's no future in that. Besides, if you get a group together by telephone and get reviewed, what good is a review of a group you'll never use again? How are you going to get a record deal if you don't have a concept for a record, together with some music and a band to play it? And then there is no use in making a record, if it doesn't lead to another one or to job offers. If you don't have a card with your phone number on it, how is somebody going to call you up? And what if you don't have a phone?

"I keep thinking, if *I* can have a career, why shouldn't somebody who has a talent like playing music? But it's hard to think in terms of concept and future when you can't pay your rent. Often musicians will tell me about a gig for which they were offered so much money. I say, 'That's not enough. Really, you shouldn't take it.' But you can't advise somebody not to take a record deal for bad money and bad royalty rates, or a gig for little money, if they can't pay their phone bill or buy food. People will take advantage of people who are hungry. If you need a gig badly, people will underpay you. If you're a junkie and you need the money, you'll do a record for $200. But a record is forever." Jazz may, as Mary Lou Williams has said, "heal you when you're sick," but it won't necessarily feed you when you're hungry. Maxine Gregg is dedicated to changing that situation.

TOMMY FLANAGAN

"**I**'ve finished that stint with her. It wasn't a
contract or anything. It just ended up about ten years—
sounds like it was contracted, but we just came to a
parting of the ways." A soft-spoken and thoughtful
man, pianist Tommy Flanagan paused in our conversation as he and his wife Diana tried to decide whether
there was "love lost" between Ella Fitzgerald and her
accompanist since 1968. A participant in some of the
most important recording sessions of the '50s and '60s,
a pianist who's been inspired by Bud Powell and has
mastered the difficult art of bebop piano, Flanagan was
and is a talented accompanist. But Ella Fitzgerald's
routines, Flanagan's infrequent solo opportunities,
and finally the grind of keeping up with the singer's
incessant performing schedule soured Flanagan on his
secondary role. After a mild heart attack in March of
1978, Flanagan resolved to change his life: "I was
smoking, drinking, and never thinking, as if there was
no tomorrow." Now he is performing and recording as
a soloist, and he feels that he is on the right track. I
talked to Flanagan in a hotel room in Salem,
Massachusetts. For a week he had spent his afternoons
watching tourists stumble across the street and back
between the Salem Witch Museum and the parking lot
of the Hawthorn Inn. "I'm beginning to feel," he said,

"as if I'm the only one in town who knows where he's going."

Flanagan is usually described as "professorial" by people who have had little to do with academics. Bald, with just a fringe of gray hair, Flanagan compensates with a full moustache and a hint of a goatee. Impeccably tailored, he lets his square wire-rimmed glasses fall forward at a rakish angle. In conversation he seems to peer over them at you with eyebrows upraised in an expression of perpetual kindly surprise. He is a master of the self-deprecating story: he got his first major gig at Birdland one night when Bud Powell "got lost," and recently he has had so many record offers that he "hasn't a thing to play for anybody." Nevertheless, musicians know him as one of the best of the bebop pianists, but also as a gentle man influenced by Billy Strayhorn, Ellington's "Sweet Pea." In the late '50s Flanagan recorded "Vierd Blues" with Miles Davis, *Giant Steps* with John Coltrane, and the *Saxophone Colossus* album with Sonny Rollins. Still, Flanagan's favorite examples of his own work are the mellow ballad performances made with the older Coleman Hawkins around 1960. One-time Dixieland clarinetist Pee Wee Russell called Tommy Flanagan one of the best pianists he had ever worked with. Even the apocryphal story, perpetuated in Leonard Feather's *Encyclopedia*, that the fifteen-year-old Flanagan played with Dexter Gordon, suggests the respect tendered the pianist by other musicians. "Donald Byrd or somebody made it up," Flanagan said.

Flanagan was born in 1930 in Detroit, a city dominated by General Motors but enlivened by plenty of music. To some young people, performing offered the only alternative to the factories, and a large number of first rate jazz musicians grew up there at about the same time: pianists Barry Harris and Roland Hanna, drummer Elvin Jones and his brothers Hank and Thad, guitarist Kenny Burrell, saxophonist Billy Mitchell. "There was a lot of playing in Detroit—a lot of pianos. It didn't matter what part of town. If anybody in the house played an instrument, they also had a piano.

Tommy Flanagan *by Michael Ullman*

There was always a place to have a session, whether it was my house or not. We used to play with Kenny, or at Barry Harris's." Perhaps the relative unattractiveness of the city had something to do with the dedication of these talented young people. "Everybody in Detroit was fairly advanced. Most of us wanted to get out of that place."

Flanagan's parents were interested in music, but brother Johnson Jr. was his first model: "My older brother became a professional piano player—he's not playing too much now. But he inspired me—that's where I started. He played professionally as Jay Johnson. He brought home the records I heard—Fats Waller, Teddy Wilson, Art Tatum, Billie Holiday. He took me to see the first live jazz music at the Paradise Room: I saw Fats Waller when I was ten and Jimmie Lunceford, and Erskine Hawkins." Flanagan caught the end of the era when visiting big bands put on large stage shows at neighborhood theaters. Throughout the '40s nightclubs—better adapted to the smaller ensembles of bebop—began taking over the business as the theaters folded. Flanagan had the same teacher as his brother and Barry Harris: Gladys Dillard, now in her seventies, but still teaching. The Detroit public schools offered excellent training: "They took an interest in kids who showed talent. They pushed them on. They would teach you basics. There were even good teachers in the intermediate schools. When you left junior high school there was an excellent high school." Donald Byrd went to Cass Technical "where you could major in music." Flanagan and Roland Hanna went with altoist Sonny Red to Northern.

Flanagan's music earned him money remarkably early. "I've been making a living playing the piano since I was about twelve. I had this moustache—I passed real easy. I played some gigs with my brother— some of my first dates were on clarinet and saxophone. I was playing in a club when I was fifteen. My parents didn't know. I wasn't even supposed to be up that late. By the time I was out of high school I had played some steady gigs—at the Parrot Lounge with Rudy Rutherford, for one. At another place I accompanied a singer for the first time—Bobby Caston. She had a real fast vibrato and two hits in the local area: she was doing 'God Bless the Child' and 'Call Me Darling.' I dug working with her. I would play fifteen minutes with a bassist, and then she would come in."

Flanagan is most animated when talking about other musicians. Much of his youth seems to have been spent sneaking out of the house and into clubs. "When I was a teenager a cat said 'Art Tatum's going to be at this place—he goes there every night.' So I went there and sure enough he came around four o'clock. I was supposed to be in bed. He didn't sit down to play until about five in the morning. He played a couple hours. That was his routine, playing until maybe early in the afternoon. Then he'd go to sleep. That was my hero." He first met Tatum by chance, though. He remembers the occasion with glee: "I was accompanying Bobby Caston one night. I looked up and there sitting just opposite the piano at the bar was Art Tatum. I was about eighteen. There he was. He liked Bobby Caston's singing. He had played for her before. He loved playing for singers. I don't know why—he played all through them. They loved him too. I was afraid to talk to him. I met him about six times and never knew what to say. I called him Mr. Tatum. But he was very nice to me. He had a lot of patience. He stood around and listened to these young people play. He listened, and he'd say things like 'There's some rare boys in here tonight.' You knew you were going to get wiped out as soon as he sat near the piano. But it was beautiful just to be around him—just to watch him—so effortless. A drink in one hand and playing more than I could ever play in my life with the other. That was Detroit in the after-hours places."

Art Tatum's seamless style, exotic, dramatic and founded on an enormous technique, was essentially inimitable. But Bud Powell's style—strong, intense and rhythmically vital, even manic at times—was more influential on the young Flanagan, especially as it was humanized through the playing of Hank Jones and others. "I heard Bud by accident when I saw a Cootie Williams band. [Powell played with this band in 1943 and 1944.] I never heard his style of piano playing before—that forceful. I found out only later who it was. I wanted to hear that pianist again, and someone said, 'That was Bud Powell.' He hadn't recorded very much. I heard one thing—with Cootie Williams. He was one of my influences: Bud, and Hank Jones in the more modern type."

Still a teenager, Flanagan played with musicians who later became famous. He first heard the new music, bebop, through Lucky Thompson, the tenor player on some of Charlie Parker's Dial dates, and "one of the first guys that came back from New York and lived in Detroit." Later Flanagan played with Charlie Parker. As he tells it, Flanagan was with Billy Mitchell's group: "We used to do a Saturday night concert at the Broadway Capitol Theater. Every Saturday night, Billy Mitchell had about an eight-piece group. There was a disc jockey there, and they used to have a celebrity each week. This week the surprise guest was Charlie 'Bird' Parker. Everybody sat up—it couldn't be the Bird. Sure enough Bird walks up. We didn't know what to play. I was stumbling through the intro of 'Ornithology.' He played two choruses and everybody was like looking at each other—who was going to play next? Billy Mitchell was strong enough— he just barreled in there. I don't think I took a solo all night."

Flanagan didn't leave for New York until 1956. He had already played with many of the major musicians of the period and had no trouble establishing himself in this new environment. "Already there were a lot of Detroiters gone through with Basie's band—Billy Mitchell, Thad Jones, Frank Foster, and Elvin was with Bud Powell at the time. It was like a welcoming thing— another Detroiter. We had a lot of jam sessions. There were five or six clubs, mostly in Harlem, where you could go to jam every night of the week. There was the 125; Small's had a night; Basie's club. Then there was Birdland, which had Monday night sessions—I made a lot of those—and Minton's. It's nothing like that now. There's no place for young players who come to New York."

As a result of his Detroit experiences, Flanagan was called to his first important recording session; with a Miles Davis group featuring Sonny Rollins, he cut two blues, "No Line" and "Vierd Blues," and surprisingly, a ballad by Dave Brubeck, "In Your Own Sweet Way." "It was my birthday; that's how I remember. My twenty-sixth birthday. March 16. Miles had lived in Detroit for a few years before he got his quintet with Coltrane and Philly Joe together. I played with him in Detroit at the Bluebird Inn. That was Billy Mitchell's gig, and Miles was like a guest artist for a couple of months. He was going through a period of straightening himself out. Everybody knew him because of Bird. He wrote lots of songs then—'Four' and 'Tune-up.' He had the date and I got the call. We just cooked. All except that one Brubeck tune. That came about strangely. Miles had that tune in his back pocket—a sketch of the chords. I remember him telling me how to voice the intro. He always knows exactly what he wants. It makes him easy to work with. If you don't play what he wants, he tells you like this [whispering hoarsely]—'Play block chords, but not like Milt Buckner. In the style of Ahmad Jamal.' I didn't really get into it too much, but Red Garland really grasped that. I love Ahmad's playing, but I didn't want to play like him." Flanagan's relative intransigence on this issue probably resulted in Garland's becoming Davis's regular pianist, for Miles was entranced at the time by Jamal's crystalline sound, then the rage in certain sophisticated circles. Flanagan understands: "I know what Miles likes about it—he plays that way himself. With the space—it just gives you a lot of room to play inside of. Like Ahmad can repeat a phrase to death, but with taste. Not the kind of monotony that really wears on your nerves—he gets a lot of good out of it. The *Miles Ahead* album was almost a copy of what Ahmad recorded with a trio."

Several months after the Davis date, Flanagan was

back in the studios with Sonny Rollins for *Saxophone Colossus*. Rollins remains one of the pianist's favorite people, "a sweet guy" who, according to Flanagan, is coping with his stardom by appearing more unapproachable than he really is. Flanagan met Rollins when the latter came through Detroit with the famous Max Roach-Clifford Brown Quintet. Flanagan responds to Rollins's musical humor, though like the rest of us he grapples with the question whether Rollins knows how funny he can be. "He's serious. He's so serious at times musically that it's funny. I don't know that it's conscious that he plays funny. It sounds funny to me. For instance, 'If Ever I Would Leave You'—when I first heard it, I was on the floor laughing. But I thought he was dead serious about it. He can play a lot of different ways, but I didn't know at the time that he played that West Indian kind of flavor. Very fast vibrato—almost like a beginner's sound. Like overblowing his horn to the point where it didn't have a sound at all. But I don't know anybody that plays more musically than he does."

Flanagan accompanied Ella Fitzgerald for the first time in 1956, taking over from another pianist at the end of one of her tours. He also recorded with Thad Jones and, early in the next year, with Kenny Burrell and J. J. Johnson. While touring with Johnson, Flanagan made his first record under his own name, still in print as *The Tommy Flanagan Trio Overseas*. (Typically he responds to questions about this album bemusedly: "It's so old—it always seems funny when people seem to like it.") The date was proposed to Flanagan while he was still in New York. Having decided immediately that he would do Billy Strayhorn's "Chelsea Bridge," he ran into Strayhorn in the street and went up and introduced himself. Strayhorn took him up to his publishers and gave him a stack of all his published compositions. "I appreciated that, getting it straight from the source." Flanagan paid him back with a relatively bouncy version of "Chelsea Bridge" and, more recently, with a whole album of Strayhorn-Ellington tunes.

In the late '50s, Flanagan played with a variety of musicians, including a weekend with another hero of his, Lester Young. He had previously socialized with Lester, though in a self-effacing way: "Whenever anyone—usually a tenor player—was going to see Lester, I'd go along. He was so funny. He looked funny: he had the first natural hair cut I had ever seen. He walked funny: he sort of swayed from side to side and he shuffled." And of course he talked funny, inventing words and calling everyone "Prez." Flanagan remembers one visit when he and a friend knocked for a long time at Young's hotel room. Finally Prez answered the door, dressed only in leopard skin briefs. When he stood up in the window to pull down a blind, he stopped traffic on Broadway. Flanagan played with Young at Gem's Paradise in Brooklyn six months before the tenor saxophonist died. They were accompanied by the unfortunate drumming of Willie Jones, a man who looked as cool as Max Roach, but who didn't keep much of a beat. "Prez looked bad, but he had looked bad so long we didn't know the end was so near. His face was pale—no color—but he had a beautiful pork-pie hat on."

In 1959, Flanagan participated in Coltrane's first session on Atlantic: they recorded "Giant Steps," "Cousin Mary" and others. Coltrane was in a transitional period. He had recorded *Kind of Blue* with Miles Davis and was soon to put together the quartet with McCoy Tyner, Jimmy Garrison and Elvin Jones. Using a technique learned from Miles Davis, Coltrane turned up with a whole range of new tunes—in his characteristic manner trying to ensure spontaneity by presenting his musicians with unfamiliar material. He also brought along some tunes he wanted to forget. "As he explained it to me, in this date he wanted to get a lot of things out of his system. He did a lot of songs with that same kind of chord progression as in 'Giant Steps.' Some things didn't even appear on the record—we just couldn't play them. The tempos were too fast and we didn't have enough time to get it down in one session. Why they like to do a whole album in one session I don't know. It almost kills you. To stay with that kind of playing—so intense—for eight hours a day. It takes its toll on you, unless you really know what you are doing. Trane knew what *he* was doing." By implication, on this date Flanagan didn't always know, and his solo in "Giant Steps," praised by Nat Hentoff for its use of space, seems to me one of the few places on record where Flanagan betrays insecurity: it trails away limply until overtaken by a forceful Coltrane.

Coltrane did get those tunes out of his system. "I never heard him play 'Giant Steps' in person. It was just something he had to record. He put it down and forgot about it. He did use that format with other songs. It was a little irregular—like a song usually relates a minor 7th to a 7th to a major. Well, Trane might have things going major-major-major. It made you think a little different, if you weren't ready for it. If the tempo was fast, you *couldn't* think of it. *Giant Steps* was like that. It made it exciting, especially when he'd say, 'Okay, you got it.' "

Having worked with Coleman Hawkins, Flanagan was back with Ella Fitzgerald from 1963-65, and then again from 1968-78. He left her partially because he needed more time to himself—Fitzgerald's schedule is hectic. "When I first started working with Ella, we worked forty to forty-five weeks out of the year. There wasn't much time for anything else. She would take a couple of weeks at Christmas and a month in the summer—until recently, when she had trouble with her eyes. She's cut down quite a bit—not because she wants to." Himself relatively retiring, Flanagan says wonderingly of Fitzgerald, "She just loves it; there's nothing like applause."

Flanagan feared that he was getting stale in his accompaniments: "Her repertoire can't change that much because she is identified with certain things. What she likes to do is really be current—do commercial things. That's okay, but I don't care for that myself." A modest man, Flanagan can be a percussive player: his improvisations flow gracefully over a steady pulse, but his phrases have the brisk accents, subtle delays and sudden rushes that enliven the best bebop choruses. He is melodically inventive, and both gracious and tactful in ensemble playing.

Despite his recent heart attack, Flanagan's solo career is back on track. He has played at Michael's Pub and Bradley's in New York, and joined fellow beboppers Barry Harris and Walter Davis in an exciting "Piano Pinnacle" concert in Cami Hall. Chuck Israel's National Jazz Ensemble presented a concert featuring Flanagan; as a surprise, they arranged his "Delarna" for a big band. At the piano Flanagan is serious, but zestful, poised and intelligent—"at ease," as the title of one of his recordings suggests. He knows what he wants to do: play the best compositions of Ellington, Strayhorn, the beboppers and of Tommy Flanagan, too. "I like bebop. It takes a long time to learn how to play that music. I guess I'll always be playing it. That's the music I love best, except for some of the things I hope to write myself. I'll have more time to do it now." Now is his time for the spotlight.

RAHSAAN ROLAND KIRK

Before Rahsaan Roland Kirk died at the age of forty-one, he had recorded tributes to Fats Waller, Billie Holiday, Duke Ellington, Lester Young, Thelonious Monk, Sidney Bechet, Don Byas, Roy Haynes, Charles Mingus, Clifford Brown, Barney Bigard and John Coltrane. Known for his astonishing ability to play as many as three instruments at the same time, often with at least one in tune, Kirk was an aggressive publicist of the whole tradition of black music: he would surprise a hip audience by picking up a clarinet and playing a reckless, dotty solo in the style of old New Orleans, and, while touring with the rock band The Who in the '60s, he regularly lectured his youthful admirers on the dangers of electronics. If things go on the way they have been, he would say, people will have to plug themselves in to make love. He loved to lecture, heckle and inveigh: the cover of one of his albums tells us "You Must Read The Back of This Album," and the title of another is *Prepare Yourself to Deal With a Miracle*. He liked to talk about love and sing about sex—come on baby, he would plead, let me shake your tree. I would say that he often had his tongue in his cheek, except that it is difficult to predict where might be the tongue of a man who plays three instruments simultaneously. In a small dark room in Detroit, named the Ibo Cultural Center by someone with an inflated view of his club or a dismal vision of the future of the Ibos, I heard Kirk lecture the already convinced audience about the need to support black composers. Earlier he had played a duet with a tambourine player, demonstrating that black music need not rely on electronic gimmickry. He noted that black composers—even those as prominent as Ellington—do not receive enough attention, and that black musicians and audiences must take the responsibility for publicizing them. Then he played a medley of Gershwin tunes.

Born in Columbus, Ohio, in 1936 and blinded soon after, Kirk said that the idea of playing several instruments at the same time came to him in a dream. Along with the tenor sax, he learned to play two obscure saxophones called the manzello and stritch, thin-sounding relatives of the alto and the soprano. Since then, Kirk has been recorded playing the clarinet, flute and piccolo, English horn, harmonium, and a variety of other instruments, including bells, gongs, whistles, sirens and cymbals. He invented an instrument by taking the bell of a trombone and attaching a reed mouthpiece. He played the nose flute— one would rather hear about it than see it played—and he prefaced his "Fly Town Nose Blues" by mentioning how few of us, cocaine addicts excepted, ever do anything for our noses.

Kirk made his first album in 1956 for the King label, an organization with limited distribution that did little for his career. In 1960 he began to make a name for himself when he recorded for the Chicago label Argo. Immediately the recording created controversy, and soon Kirk was condemned by those uncomfortable with the vaudeville aspects of his performances. In 1963 a disgruntled Leroi Jones wrote about the New York nightclub, The Five Spot: "In a city that is just bursting at the seams with young cooking musicians, the Spot seemed content to lay with Roland Kirk" (Black Music). Kirk was twenty-seven at the time, and had been before a large public for less than three years, but Jones talked about him as if he were old and

Rahsaan Roland Kirk *by Andy Freeberg/Encore*

established. Jones was offended when he saw Kirk spin a bass on his head while holding a note on the saxophone.

But the Argo record is relatively restrained, featuring Kirk playing multiple instruments only occasionally, as at the beginning of "The Call." The record is notable for Kirk's gentle version of "Our Love Is Here to Stay," and for the relaxed "Our Waltz." At this point Kirk sounded like a mainstream player who remained unaffected by the new waves of Ornette Coleman, Cecil Taylor or even, for that matter, John Coltrane.

The gospel influence evident in "Spirit Girl" on the Argo album was also being exploited by Charles Mingus at the same time, and "Spirit Girl," with its developing call and response patterns, makes Kirk's move to Mingus's band in 1961 seem inevitable. Kirk made *Oh Yeah* with Mingus: many of the characteristics of this Mingus recording became typical of Kirk. "Ecclusiastics" is a Mingus tribute to his church influences: Kirk quotes "Down by the Riverside" in a solo that looks forward to his clarinet pieces in the Dixieland style. Kirk solos in the mournful Mingus tune, "Oh Lord, Dear Lord, Don't Let Them Drop That Atomic Bomb on Me," a composition whose mock-serious lyrics and melancholy melody suggest later Kirk pieces. He performs in Mingus's bumptious tribute to Fats Waller, the suggestive "Eat That Chicken." This session is emotional, as Mingus is hollering in the background; it draws on jazz traditions, commenting on them humorously; and it is striking for its loosely swinging ensemble. The music is varied and good fun.

In 1961 Kirk started recording for Mercury, a company he left in 1965 when he went to Atlantic, his recording company to the end. For Mercury he recorded "From Bechet, Byas, and Fats," his tribute to three seemingly diverse styles. Kirk explained: "This represents Sidney Bechet on manzello—not the way he would play it but with the force. The bass and piano are like Waller and the tenor like Don. I'm not trying to play any of their stuff note for note; it's the groove they put me in—the way they inspire me for what I want to write and play."

Kirk's "No Tonic Prez" demonstrates his usefulness as a commentator on jazz history. The tune is a tribute to Lester Young, the soft-toned lazy sounding tenor player who prepared the way for bop, but it is played in the style of Coltrane, whose assertive rhythm and harsh tone seem antithetical to Prez. Kirk comments: "The head doesn't have a tonic (the layman might think I'm talking about a drink). It's a riff that I heard Prez use and I extended the line to utilize all the horn, from top to bottom. I know Prez's music so I'm able to extend myself on what he has done, instead of just trying to play his licks. Coltrane does Prez-like things on the horn but he extends them." The attentive listener can hear the connection, as if Coltrane were playing Lester Young.

Influenced by jazz musicians from Fats Waller onward, Kirk continued to develop through the '60s. He relinquished no instrument or style. Eclectic, Rahsaan (this name also came to him in a dream) had what Ira Gitler called the biggest ears in the business. Not surprisingly he could sound something like John Coltrane: he recorded a three-part tribute to Trane for Atlantic.

Kirk was the ideal festival performer. Self-involved and intense, undistracted by time limits or anxious promoters, he created his own atmosphere and possessed his own "hip vibrations," as he called them. Led on stage, he was a striking sight—a walking pawnshop, Whitney Balliett called him. Kirk's dark glasses and jutting jaw, his full lips and large build, suggested his weight and power. Yet he looked older than he was. He walked slowly but played passionately, feeling for the three saxophones and assorted smaller instruments hung constantly from his neck, moving quickly from song to song, stopping only to talk to an audience to get a sense of its mood, building toward a climax. Kirk played ballads, spirituals, and his own compositions. Given forty minutes on stage before a large audience, he would stomp, rip and roar until he got the tumultuous response he wanted.

Not every influence on Kirk was beneficial. In a reunion concert with Mingus at Carnegie Hall, Kirk listened to the post-Coltrane saxophone shrieks of Hamiet Bluiett, and thinking that this must be where it's at, responded with some unmusical squeaking of his own. Nor were all of Kirk's experiments successful. He explains on one record that he is going to play an Ellington tune and that he will himself represent all the reed parts of the Ellington band. The parts are all there, but each is rendered feebly and intermittently. On *Prepare Yourself to Deal With a Miracle*, Kirk plays for twenty or so minutes without stopping for breath— he had learned the technique of a circular breathing from Harry Carney. But the solo is annoying and tiresome.

In 1976 Kirk had a stroke that left one half of his body nearly paralyzed. Almost immediately he began playing with what he had left. No one can deny his courage or his confidence. Before he died of a second stroke, Kirk was honored by two recorded tributes: by Freddie Hubbard on *Bundle of Joy* and by Billy Hart on *Enchance*.

More tributes to Rahsaan Roland Kirk will be forthcoming. Not an avant-garde player, Kirk was an innovator only in technique. Few people will follow his lead in playing more than one instrument simultaneously or in trying to play wind instruments without breathing. Nevertheless, Kirk was a force in music: he brought a whole range of jazz styles to audiences who would never have heard them otherwise. He never stopped listening, learning and struggling. He holds many odd distinctions: *down beat* magazine had to create the category of Miscellaneous Instruments in its jazz polls in order to accommodate Kirk's offerings. And he is surely the only blind man to have been dragged off a plane as a suspected hijacker: somewhere about his body he was carrying a ceremonial knife, the airline explained. Critic Joachim Berendt said Kirk had "all the wild untutored quality of a street musician coupled with the subtlety of a modern jazz musician." That wild quality can be heard on *The Jaki Byard Experience*. On this album, Kirk solos in the gospel tune "Shine on Me" ("Let the light from the lighthouse shine on me"). There is no parody in his clarinet playing here, only joy. Kirk himself was at times competitive, perhaps even abrasive. Too often in his recording he reached for some technical trick that added little to his playing. But at its best, Kirk's music was filled with the wild spirit that informs the greatest jazz: hearing him, one can almost feel that music, like the Lord in "Shine on Me," can "heal the sick and raise the dead."

SAM RIVERS

At the end of our conversation, Sam Rivers peered past the metal gate barring the entrance to his Bond Street loft in the Soho district of New York City, smiled at his wife, and mentioned to me that once the music business had seemed too much for him, that stung by criticism and neglect he had had what amounted to a breakdown. If he was once too sensitive, Rivers is now confident and secure. One of the few musicians associated with the jazz avant-garde who works as much as he wants, he has given concerts in the converted warehouse that has been his home for almost a decade; he teaches privately; and he has had an enormous though subterranean influence on other players. His free improvisations on tenor and soprano saxophones, flute and piano have reached a loyal, though perhaps too small, public, and he has been able to perform and record his orchestral compositions. The 1978 Newport in New York Festival presented "The World of Sam Rivers" one evening in Carnegie Hall. In 1979, he presented at New York's Public Theater a piece for thirty-two musicians. Now, as Rivers told me, criticism "doesn't touch me."

His mysterious look, patchy beard and tall, thin frame clothed characteristically in something like battle fatigues, make Rivers look curiously like an elongated Che Guevara. He comes from a family of talented musicians. His grandfather, Reverend Marshall W. Taylor, collected a volume of slave songs. Rivers's father sang in the gospel Silvertone Quartet, and his mother accompanied him on piano. Born on the road in Reno, Oklahoma in 1930, Rivers was brought home to Chicago where the family lived until Rivers's father was killed in an accident. Seven years later the family moved to Little Rock. Sam's varied training in music began early. He heard spirituals and light classics at home and learned several instruments: "I was playing piano at first, then after a while violin and on top of that I was playing alto sax. When I was about ten or twelve years old I started playing soprano in the marching band." He was also singing with his brother and two cousins in a quartet called, prophetically, the "Tiny Tims"—"We had a radio thing in Little Rock. We did a half-hour every week. It was gospel, spirituals and popular music."

Rivers took up tenor sax seriously while at Jarvis Christian College in Texas. Then after graduation and a stint in the Navy, he and his brother Martin moved to Boston. "I went to study at the Boston Conservatory—composition and viola—but I was also playing violin." At night Rivers played saxophone at a small bar and grill on Essex Street across from the old RKO Theater: "All the bands used to play the RKO and then they'd come across the street and hear us play. That's how Charlie Mariano went with Stan Kenton. He was playing with me one night and Kenton heard him. A lot of musicians went out like that. Quincy Jones was in the band on trumpet, Nat Pierce playing piano, Jaki Byard also. There were three or four bands a night—never a dull moment. They'd start at noon and go to midnight. Two bands during the day and two bands at night. I was lucky—we played from seven to ten, but it was seven days a week." Even this early Rivers showed a concern for other players that is a hallmark of his career. When a hungry musician came by the grill, Rivers would let him take his place: "They'd come in and play and eat, and I'd go to the movies which

Sam Rivers *by Deborah Feingold*

were right around the corner. They'd sit in and I'd pay them."

The bar provided an apprenticeship in popular music: "There was an old barrelhouse pianist who worked there—Larry Willis. The first night I came, he just said hello and started playing. I didn't know the first tune so I just had to sit there. Because he never said anything; just played all night. We were there for about a year, so I came away with full knowledge of the standards. He knew them all and I must have learned two or three thousand standards—which I never use anymore."

For a time Rivers made a living writing jingles, an experience that still taints his view of popular songs: "I put music to lyrics. You see that thing in the paper—send your lyrics and we'll put music to it. I used to write those tunes. I was very adept. I look at song-writing as a minimal occupation. It's not really an art—it's a craft. You see a line—it suggests a melody. There's choices of course, because one sentence suggests ten melodies. You take the first that comes into your mind, so you don't get bogged down trying to be artistic about the subject. It's a product."

In Boston in the '50s Rivers was playing bebop—he was part of a big band that called themselves "The Beboppers." Nevertheless, "Lester Young was my first influence. Lester Young and Coleman Hawkins and Eddie Davis—a lot of people like that." Even so, Rivers made a point of avoiding strict imitation. He played a bebop style but not many bebop tunes. While at school he played viola in the Conservatory's orchestra. Some experiments there in contemporary classical music, he says, helped the evolution of his jazz playing. "The European [classical] avant-garde—they go a bit further than the jazz avant-garde. Throwing ink on paper and drawing graphs. We were playing paintings at the Museum. You would study the painting, its lines, and then play. The musicians were oriented toward European music—there were just a few jazz musicians, and we were invited because of our specific talents for improvising."

The early '60s marked a change in Rivers's style. He was playing classical music and performing regularly with Herb Pomeroy's Basie-ish big band, but he was also working with a group including young Tony Williams on drums and Hal Galper on piano. "We were listening to Cecil Taylor's music and Ornette's. So that opened [the music] up. It was a natural evolution for me." Rivers had been playing pieces without a set chord structure when he heard Coleman and Taylor; they confirmed the validity of Rivers's experiments. Rivers considers this break away from strict rhythms and the chord structure of songs, typified by Ornette Coleman's and Cecil Taylor's music, the most radical innovation in music in the last fifty years—perhaps the last radical innovation.

On the road with blues singer T-Bone Walker in 1964, Rivers was asked to join the Miles Davis quintet. He played with Davis a scant six months: "It was supposed to have been Wayne Shorter working with Miles and I was supposed to go with Art Blakey. I just decided I didn't want to go into any more bebop. I was already past bebop." Miles has had an impact on most of the musicians who have worked with him—but the influence is not always positive. "I believe that the musicians who went through Miles's bands were just as impressed with his lifestyle as they were with his music. So if you want to achieve that kind of lifestyle, there's certain things you have to do with the music. You're not going to have it while playing at the frontiers of the music."

Soon after leaving Miles Davis, Rivers moved to New York, a change that involved some sacrifice: "I was pretty well set. It was really an uprooting to move, to sell my house and all that. I was as successful as I could be without being famous. I moved specifically because I had all these orchestrations and big band compositions, and it was hard finding musicians to play it. We had to move to Harlem." Rivers started a studio there, but needed more room, so he relocated in his current place in Soho, where in 1970 he started giving concerts. "I wanted to have a place where I could rehearse any time I wanted to. I might have to have a rehearsal at two in the morning—because musicians are working. That's impossible in any other city. I can practice and play any time I want. I started the concerts because a fellow approached me when George Wein moved the Newport thing to New York and he didn't hire New York musicians. All the young musicians who come to New York, they know about this place. I try to gather all the young musicians and find some way for them to have an outlet for their talents so they don't get discouraged."

Rivers played with Cecil Taylor from 1968-73 in an arrangement that broke off when Taylor went to teach at Antioch: "I think it's best for me, because Cecil's such an overpowering player. When I first went with him, we rehearsed four, five, six, seven hours without stopping. I really learned something about music, about what happens to you when you're there for six or seven hours. It's like a long distance runner. After a while you don't feel the pain; you don't feel anything. You've run through all your cliches. You have to deal with something new in a different way altogether. It gets to be like total creativity."

That condition is the reason for the long solos that typify modern jazz, Rivers says, solos that might offend audiences used to the two or three choruses by Louis Armstrong or Charlie Parker. But Rivers insists that he heard Parker play half-hour solos and he recalls the legendary all-night Kansas City jam sessions with such figures as Lester Young and Ben Webster. Now musicians are playing solos on the concert stage that previously would have been reserved for private sessions: "The only thing that is new is that the audience hears what used to be private among the musicians. The audience is fortunate—musicians play for the audience the way they did for themselves."

Besides producing concerts in his Bond Street loft, Rivers conducts workshops and gives lessons. He tries to instill in his students his own sense of the importance of individuality in music: "The way I'm playing I make sure that I'm not imitated. I make sure that my students come up with their own individual approaches to the music. My students write their own exercises. They don't play anything but their own music—so how are they going to copy anybody?" A well-schooled musician, Rivers wants to play intelligently and with emotion too. "The intuitive musicians don't last. They usually fall by the wayside. You really have to study. You can only do so much with intuition and then the brain has to take over, and you have to figure things." He is not interested in the kind of subtlety found in some contemporary classical music. "I can appreciate it—but I'm into fire. The emotional part of music is just as important as the cerebral. I'm not considered cerebral because of the emotion in my music. But who was more cerebral than Charlie Parker or Lester Young? The balance has to be there for it to be music." On the other hand, Rivers draws a distinction between what he calls emotion and sheer excitement. Rock music, often called "high energy," is to him merely loud. "This is the age of excitement. Everyone has got to be on a roller-coaster. But I'm not sure excitement and emotion are the same thing."

In recent years, Rivers has made a series of successful records. His tours are consistently well-received. He cares for his audiences: "There's an accessibility about our music. There's no compromise, but we still swing, we still play blues sounds, and avant-garde too. It's easy enough to identify with some part of our music. We keep it changing—it's sort of a stream of consciousness. We are all familiar with the history of the music, so we can go anywhere we want. I'm thinking in terms of creativity first. I'm also thinking in terms of change in the music. I don't want to bore anybody." A typical performance of the Sam Rivers trio might begin with a short phrase played on Rivers's even-toned tenor. Dave Holland might answer the phrase on his bass or harmonize Rivers's next statement. As the piece develops—little is planned beforehand—the two will be joined by drummer Barry Altschul, and together the musicians play nonstop for as much as an hour and a half. Rivers changes the music by suddenly playing in a blues vein, by dropping out and allowing a duet to develop, by humming and singing, and by changing instruments: in almost every appearance he plays tenor and soprano, piano and flute. Inevitably there are moments when the music drags, but also there are moments of what Rivers calls "total creativity," when the band plays spontaneously and dramatically with both soul and wit. In his live performances, Rivers feels comfortable, as he says, "starting with nothing and just building."

Curiously, his recordings are not necessarily more strictly arranged. "In a record I like a bit of plan beforehand. We talk about it—like, we're going to do a certain section here, or we're going to play for five minutes, and there'll be a duet here. That's all. Nothing else. I can do big band arrangements like that too—but I write them out. I have big band arrangements that are all written; I have some not written at all; and some, my favorites, are part written and part improvised. I see that some people criticize the densities in my music. They don't point out that these densities are built up to from one-line melodies which are harmonized. I might have three lines together at the same time, each harmonized. But I try to cover the spectrum so you can't really say, 'he does this.' I have the knowledge and experience and try to use all the existing materials I can. I have no set patterns of composition. When I start writing I have no idea what I'm going to write, and when I'm finished I'm amazed that I did it. But I can explain everything."

Rivers became his own producer because of the inadequacy of the working conditions elsewhere. He notes that he has developed a reputation for being difficult. "Anyone who speaks his mind and doesn't let you cheat him is difficult in this business. It's the same all over the world. In Luxembourg, a guy said to me, 'Mr. Rivers, please do us a favor. We've got a small place and we're trying to get this jazz thing started in Luxembourg. It's a small place—if you play, we can pay you like $400.' So I looked at my schedule and I said, 'Well, we can do it since we're coming through anyway.' So we drove up from Paris, we got into the place and there's a thousand people there. I said, 'Wait a minute. We don't play.' I got up and made a speech, and told the people what was happening. People had come from miles around, from several countries and they understood. They were on my side. They paid $7 a head. The producer came up with some money, we played, but he put the word around—don't deal with Rivers; he's difficult."

It's very foul out there in the music business—it's politics and as dirty as politics can be. But it's not the musicians. It's the people that are around the music. They create a competitiveness that is not really necessary. The worst people are presidents of recording companies. Agents are terrible. I'm thinking of one cat—he wanted to be a drummer and he was the worst in the world. Musicians would laugh at him. So he decided to get an agent and six or eight months later, he was saying 'I can get these cats a dime a dozen.' I'm shocked at this kind of talk." Rivers played in Washington at a club whose owner asked him to play for thirty minutes and take an hour break so that customers would drink more. Rivers is equally disenchanted with the record business. He has terminated an agreement with ABC Impulse Records, partially because he felt they were not giving him adequate publicity or studio time. "I made *Crystals* (a big band record) in three hours in the studio. That's phenomenal. I didn't have enough studio time really to do a good record."

Recently, Rivers cut back on the activities he was managing at his loft. "I had students coming in from eleven o'clock and workshops going as late as six— then the concert would start around eight and two or three groups would play until four in the morning. It was really a bit much." Only his concern for other musicians kept him going: "There was nothing else, no other place to play, so I couldn't break it off." Every year the loft was open, Rivers lost money despite foundation and state grants. "The place was too small—it can hold 125-130 people at the most. And if I have two bands and am paying $500 a band, there's no way I can make $1000 at the door unless I'm charging $10 a head. Even that wouldn't cover the newspapers and the telephone and the flyers."

Rivers is the first to admit that he will never be a superstar—he is not even a cult figure, because "you really can't copy my way of soloing." But even at its most aggressive his playing has an indefinable charm. He is a responsible man: "I've never been late. I've never played an uninspired performance." And he clearly believes in the power of music: "You can write about a person whatever you like but in the final results, it is up to that person. If he doesn't come up with it—no matter what you write—he's not going to last." Perhaps we cannot touch Sam Rivers, but a growing number of people are finding that Rivers can touch them. He's lasting.

JOHN SNYDER

The history of jazz recording is, to an extent larger than generally realized, a history of jazz producers. These are the men and women who come up with the money to make the record in the first place, and often they decide who will be in the band, what tunes will be performed, and in what style they will be played. The results may be misleading. People who are entranced by the pure tone and lilting swing of Bix Biederbecke's jazz age cornet may be distressed by the cornball tunes over which he flung his solos: it is reassuring to hear that some of the tunes were imposed by producers or artist and repertoire men such as the bull-headed Eddie King of RCA Victor Records. Even today some producers create "jam sessions" in which musicians who would pass each other by in the street show little attraction for one another on the stage or in the studio.

Naturally, recording companies want to reach the widest possible audience, and hence the tendency to throw musicians of different musical backgrounds together to play something called jazz-rock—a musical fusion that often consists of boring riffs played over the mechanical rhythms of a drum that thumps like a heart in trouble and an electric bass with three notes. Whereas musicians of the '20s had to put up with the feigned sentimentality of their hard-nosed producers, the pop-jazz player of today has merely to suffer the aggressive tedium of a music designed to make cheap loudspeakers sound good.

These trends should make us cherish conscientious producers who feel that their job is to find an audience rather than to mold an artist. One such businessman is John Snyder, the head of Artists House Records, an organization designed to "make the company work for the artist, rather than the other way around." Previously with CTI and A&M, Snyder is a fair-haired North Carolinian living in New York City. He has a southern accent and a sharp point of view. His dedication to the artist has been called naively idealistic by others in the industry. When A&M Records pulled out of the Horizon label directed by Snyder, Arista's Steve Backer said that the effect of this decision by a major record company would hurt jazz. Backer told *Downbeat*'s Chuck Berg: "They [at A&M] naively assumed that a large production budget, expensive packaging and some good music would have to result in great sales. They simply weren't realistic in terms of what they could expect in sales from the artists they were recording, and a year down the line found themselves enormously in debt, and, man, we all felt the impact." Today Snyder would suggest that the expectations of A&M were confused rather than inflated, and he would quarrel with the suggestion that the Horizon line lost a lot of money. Snyder certainly felt that the company wasted money—but he still believes in good music and elegant packaging. He has developed the surface cynicism of an idealist who has been bounced around but at the same time gained considerable insight into the musicians who are his friends—among them Ornette Coleman, Chet Baker, Jim Hall and the late Paul Desmond. He told me: "I don't have any commitment to the idea of music, or the history of it. My commitment, if that is even the right word, is to people—the people who are making the record and the people who are going to buy the record."

In his apartment overlooking Rockefeller University and the East River, I talked to Snyder about his

John Snyder *by Deborah Feingold*

career, his company and his friends. When in 1973 Snyder was unenthusiastically finishing law school in Chapel Hill, North Carolina, he wrote Creed Taylor of CTI Records, then a successful high-priced jazz record label, asking Taylor for a job. Snyder, a trumpeter whose idols included Chet Baker, Miles Davis and, previously, Al Hirt, had been a music education major in college. He admired CTI's products—their clear sound, suave arrangements and all-star soloists—and he talked his way into their employ. Once at CTI he was exposed to different facets of the record business. "I was obviously a young, naive, excited kid who had a pretty good education and was highly motivated. So he hired me. At the beginning my job was publishing and A&R. I would listen to all the tapes that came in. I would approve test pressings. I would edit some singles. Later, Creed involved me in every area of the record business. He came in the office one day and he said, 'Would you like to be involved in production?' I said, 'What is production?' Well, production turns out to be manufacturing, that is to say, supervising the manufacture of the records and the jackets. CTI had a very involved manufacturing problem, because Creed didn't just print on the cardboard jacket and slip a record into it. He had a picture printed on paper at a place in Connecticut that printed art books. It cost him sixty cents just for this piece of paper and most record companies pay twelve cents for the whole jacket. No wonder CTI had the image they did. They paid for it. And you did too if you bought their records."

At CTI Snyder was thrilled to be around musicians he respected but surprised to see the way they were manipulated by the recording process. Creed Taylor had a sound in mind, and his musicians adapted to his idea. "When I bought records and wasn't in the record business, my favorite label was CTI. I admired the slickness of it and the good sound, and I felt that I could depend on it. But when I found out the conditions under which those records were made, I felt that I had been had.

"The musicians weren't having any fun, and the

records did not reflect the artists in an honest, transparent way. George Benson told me that when he made *White Rabbit* he had driven all night from Detroit. When he got there, [arranger] Don Sebesky presented him with tunes that Benson didn't know, and consequently played tentatively. After the session, Creed told Sebesky to fill in the gaps. Now I liked *White Rabbit*. But I know that it is not a clear artistic image of George Benson. It's different from an artist having a vision and being able to bring it forth for other people to see it. Taylor was successful in exposing jazz artists to an audience twenty or thirty times larger than they had been exposed to before. This talent eventually cost him the loyalty of the musicians who went on to record for 'major' labels as soon as their CTI contracts expired."

When CTI was forced to retrench, Creed Taylor fired Snyder in a friendly way, telling him that the company would not be picking up the options on Jim Hall and Paul Desmond. Snyder brought this information and a lot of plans to A&M, where he was hired to create the prestigious Horizon label. As it developed, Horizon was impressive for its sheer variety of recordings, from several albums with the brash, cheerful-sounding big band of Thad Jones and Mel Lewis to two collections of deeply felt duets by bassist Charlie Haden playing with Ornette Coleman, Keith Jarrett, Alice Coltrane and others. The best-selling Horizon record featured the duets of Dave Brubeck and Paul Desmond. Horizon also produced the first Ornette Coleman recording with electric instruments and a striking group of Jim Hall performances called *Commitment*. In the liner notes to that album, Hall says: "We didn't want just another slick jazz record. The whole idea of the album was to work with friends, using exactly who I wanted, and make a *personal* statement." Critic J. R. Taylor adds, "There is perhaps no way effectively to 'produce' such a talent, except by giving it a musical choice and room to run." But it takes more than freedom to capture even a "personal statement," and Taylor's comment denies perhaps too strongly the contribution of the producer.

Horizon albums also proved Snyder's and his associates' respect for the audience. All the Horizon albums contained selected discographies of the artists involved, full details on personnel and recording dates, and even sketches of arrangements or transcriptions of solos. For instance, *Commitment* offers a sketch of Hall's "Walk Soft" and of "Lament for a Fallen Matador" as well as a transcription of the guitarist's solo on Victor Herbert's "Indian Summer."

Snyder felt that he had a mandate to produce a line of important, although perhaps not strikingly lucrative, recordings. Perhaps he felt, as Steve Backer suggested, that high quality recordings packaged well *must* be profitable. At any rate, Snyder insists that the Horizon line as a whole did not lose money. Snyder was fired the day he presented A&M executive Jerry Moss with a clock made from a Horizon record by the Revolutionary Jazz Ensemble. Having heard of Moss's allegedly extreme reaction to this avant-garde set, he meant to make a joke about its poor sales.

Snyder started Artists House with several clear-cut goals. He would "facilitate the trip from artist to consumer" of some important music. He would ensure that "each Artist House record is as clear an idea of the artist as can be given and that it is totally controlled and approved by the artist," and that each record is manufactured according to as high a standard as possible. And Snyder hoped to give his artist friends a better deal. "Originally the motivation was really people, three people—Chet Baker, Ornette Coleman and Jim Hall. I wanted to reverse the roles of record company and artist, so that the record company would work for the artist."

Snyder notes that it is difficult for most jazz artists to make a living from performing. In recent years Ornette Coleman has been playing in this country only once a year: at the Newport in New York Festival. An artist like Chet Baker is lucky to appear in clubs in four or five cities a year, making $1500 for the week, which he has to split with his sidemen. Not surprisingly, many serious jazz musicians look to recordings for their sustenance.

But a recording contract with a major record label does not necessarily mean financial security. In Snyder's experience, a contract might stipulate that the artist get a royalty of 5 percent of the retail price of the records. Typically, however, the artist is paid a royalty on only 90 percent of the records sold—a provision created in the days when the records were made of shellac and tended to break. From that 90 percent another 15 percent is subtracted for container costs and another 30 percent for what are called "free goods." (That is, three hundred albums will be given to a distributor for every thousand he buys. The distributor pays for these free goods by paying a proportionately higher wholesale price for the records he pays for.) The system can be used to deprive the artist of royalties. Only the artist loses because, according to his contract, he is paid a percentage of the list price on what might come out to be as few as half of the records manufactured under his name.

Music publishers, the people who license the compositions played on any given record, rebelled against this system: "Five years or so ago, the Harry Fox Agency, which represents a great many publishers, insisted on being paid for every record that goes into a retail store. The publishers are paid on every record now, but the artists, because they have no one organization that represents their interests, are subject to whatever record companies give them. Often the free goods provision is hidden in the contract: that is to say, the provision is couched in terms such as 'the record company may supply merchandise to distributors for certain merchandising plans.' But that means the company can give away anything they want to." The artist may also be asked to pay recording costs. The system is sufficiently complicated that many artists don't understand the contracts they sign.

The Artists House contract is simple but relatively expensive for the company. First of all, Artists House does not buy the music from the artist; it leases the rights to the recordings for five years, after which time the rights revert to the artist. This procedure eliminates one problem many musicians complain of: their recordings may be deleted by a company, never to surface again despite a steady though perhaps small demand for the music. More important perhaps, Snyder pays the artist 67.5 cents for every record pressed. There are no deductions, although, as Snyder says, "I am sure if we had some industry people sitting here they would argue for free goods, saying that they are necessary to sell records." This system means that the company pays royalties on records sent free to reviewers.

At this point the company can only succeed with established musicians who have "devoted fans." Snyder speculates—I think optimistically—about guitarist Jim Hall: "I believe that the market will stand maybe three or four Jim Hall records a year. I think there are 25,000 diehard Jim Hall fans out there and they're going to buy everything. If that is true, if we can sell 100,000 Jim Hall records a year, he can make $67,500 in royalties. The interesting point is that since record company contracts are the way they are and since my contract is the way it is, I only have to sell a fifth the number of records for the artist to make the same amount of money."

Snyder has taken steps to ensure that the consumer who buys an Artists House record will be satisfied at least with its manufacture. The records are pressed on the best vinyl: "Each record costs about 65 cents because it's on virgin vinyl. There are three kinds of vinyl. Virgin vinyl has never been used before. Pure vinyl has no additives: when a record is stamped there might be a trim that comes off the edge of the record. That trim is collected mechanically and is added to virgin vinyl to make what they call pure vinyl. Most pop records are made out of vinyl with additives in it, which increase the surface noise. I've had a lot of trouble with my pressings: in fact, I had four different pressing plants before I ever got any records out." The jackets are carefully designed and the sleeves contain the kind of useful information found on Horizon records.

"There's only one general characteristic I'd like for the series," says Snyder, "and that is that it's going to be dependable. We've made every attempt to capture the music of an artist who people think is important and who is serious about what he is doing. We guarantee the record was not made under time pressure, the way most jazz albums are. I don't want to dominate the music. I don't want the music to express my personality, although I have an obvious relationship to it."

Consistently Snyder talks about himself as a middleman who is lucky enough to be able to make money by using an artist's own strengths and talents. Jazz musicians need the producer: "Good producing is a collaboration between the artist and the producer. There are as many other ways of producing as there are producers. And unlike many artistic endeavors, to create *recorded* art almost requires a producer. The producer is the first audience. The better the producer is, the more pure, critical, direct and understandable his observations will be. And it helps to be fast. Capturing the artist is one of those magic moments that no one can explain but we all can recognize; that's the challenge. Of course these moments can happen in *any* music, but 'jazz' is a head-long rush for them. Going for the unknown one way or another.

"That means risks, and a high degree of failure. One reason jazz isn't played more on the radio is that most jazz records are boring. The recording method, circumstances, time, etc., is the only way I, as a producer, can affect the environment, which may facilitate the occurrence of one of these moments. Given the fact that 99 percent of all jazz recordings are negatively affected by time pressures, by incompetent producers, engineers, A&R people, and record company presidents, and the fact that the artist is getting (gotten, going to be) ripped off financially, it seems that by eliminating these problems, the success rate for jazz records, musically and commercially, would be increased. And after the expense and effort, why not present it like the special music it is?

"Nevertheless, promoters approach artists and say, 'We want you to do this, play this time for this amount of money.' They have a concept and they choose the players to fit their concept. The editor of a prominent Japanese jazz magazine invited Ornette Coleman to go to Japan, but only as a solo player—without his group. He knows that Anthony Braxton plays solo, so he insists that Ornette Coleman do it. He has no idea what Ornette wants, what Ornette thinks, or what Ornette stands for. Wouldn't we all be better off asking people like Coleman who have something to say, 'How can we help you say it in the clearest way you can?' "

Talking about Ornette leads Snyder to the reason he is staying in such a risky and troublesome business. "Ornette can walk into a room of people and in very little time read those people, and he can make anybody feel better than they felt before. Or worse, if he's talking about a problem, there's nobody who can make you cry quicker. But his uniqueness as a human being is due to his very considerate and kind approach to other people. It's really amazing. And that's why I like to be associated with him. That's why I want to help him do what he wants to do.

"I like talking to Ornette. He's got a clear view of life and he'll cut right through. I only know a few people like that, but the people who get closest to it, it seems to me, are jazz musicians. Like Chet, for all his bullshit, for all his self-abuse, he has got an amazing perception of what I can only call the truth. I know that's vague, but what I mean is, it's just an objective, humane way of being."

It remains to be seen whether this "objective, humane way of being" can be the basis for a successful record company. Artists House is an important experiment, an alternative to the large record companies and to the small ones created by individual artists. It is meant to provide a reasonable income for musicians without imposing on them the burden of doing business for themselves. Snyder envisions a time when Artists House will make it possible for significant jazz musicians to "get back to the business of being artists again." As he told me, almost carelessly, "I mean, what else? You've got to do something. Your life. You've got to pass the time of day. Why not do that?"

KEN McINTYRE

Born in Boston in 1931, multi-instrumentalist Ken McIntyre was raised in a house on the corner of Massachusetts and Columbus Avenues. Conveniently across the street was the Hi Hat, a prominent Boston nightclub where McIntyre heard Billie Holiday and Charlie Parker. Inspired by Parker, McIntyre became, in the early sixties, one of the important young musicians extending the range and techniques of the saxophone and of improvisation. His credentials were impeccable: he had earned a master's degree in music from the Boston Conservatory of Music, and he seemed destined to be a key figure in the modernist tradition building around Ornette Coleman, Cecil Taylor and Eric Dolphy. In 1960 McIntyre played alto sax, bass clarinet and flute on his first album as a leader. Later he recorded as oboist, saxophonist and clarinetist, supporting Cecil Taylor on the famous *Unit Structures* album. Nevertheless, after recording four albums as a leader, McIntyre "retired" from a business in which he could not make a living. Always a curious, or as he told me, a "nosy" person, McIntyre has taught in college and in the New York public school system since 1961. The last time he had a full week of work as a player was in 1963, though Steeplechase has recently recorded five of his records. McIntyre's music no longer sounds as radical as it did in 1960: our ears have adjusted, and he plays attractive West Indian tunes, an occasional stomping bebop composition, and some eerily affecting original ballads. He is cautiously optimistic about his future, although unhappy about the "marketplace" for African-American music: "I went into teaching because basically the world was not ready to hear me. I like to feel now that the world is ready."

McIntyre's problems with the marketplace have not left him unmarked: he can quote animatedly the inept twenty-year-old *down beat* review of his first record. His comments on the music profession are acidic. He is that rare but dangerous kind of man: he can be depressing without being depressed. He can tell a bitter story with zest, leaning forward hopefully when making a point and leaning back pleased when he is understood. He has close-cropped hair, a full beard, and warm, expressive eyes.

McIntyre studied classical piano as a child and young man: he heard West Indian music and Duke Ellington at home, and his father played mandolin. But it was Charlie Parker who inspired him to become a musician. "Actually some of my buddies turned me on to it. They were listening to Charlie Parker and they asked me to check it out. At first it didn't make any sense to me. I didn't know what it sounded like. But after listening for about five days, forty minutes a day after school, I finally got the message. It was a very enlightening period for me." He was stubborn enough to keep listening to a music he didn't understand because "it made sense to my buddies and I couldn't understand how something could make sense to them and not to me." Not surprisingly, McIntyre worries about the lack of opportunity today for people to hear challenging music. In the notes to one of his Steeplechase recordings, McIntyre tells the story of his initiation to Charlie Parker and adds: "And as a direct result of that listening experience I ultimately became a musician. I say this for those people who have thought that the Kontemporary [sic] African-American Music must instantaneously hit you over the head. For some this may occur; however, like so

many other aspects in life there is a nurturing and an appreciation that has to take place before acceptance as a way of life takes place." As do many other people connected with the music, McIntyre stresses the importance of radio in controlling people's tastes. In his notes he remembers nostalgically the time when record stores would let one play a record before buying it: "Unlike the late '40s and early '50s when it was permissible for the buyer of a recording to hear before purchasing a particular number, the public of today is not allowed the experience of looking through a pile of recordings by various artists and then selecting one to listen to prior to buying the recording. The option is not available for the listener to select/reject according to his/her taste, but rather the listener is held as part of the captive audience when he/she turns on the radio."

After high school McIntyre entered the Army; he spent some time in Japan, where he wrote "Sendai," a piece recorded only after twenty-three years. The G. I. Bill enabled him to continue his education after his discharge. When the Boston Conservatory refused to honor his diploma from the Boston Trade High School, "I had to go down to the Board of Education and take an examination which was like a high school equivalency. That was a shock to me. Then to the Conservatory. I was serious; I wanted to learn something, so I got as much as I could get out of it. I knew a lot already, but I didn't know that I knew a lot, so it was fascinating for me to see that much of what they explained to me was just things that I knew intuitively. It was put into a context so that I could articulate it. It helped me in teaching tremendously, because I can put things out very clearly and concisely—theoretical as well as applied concepts."

With a master's degree in music and a certificate in flute from the Boston Conservatory, McIntyre gigged around Boston, then went to New York City. One night he jammed with Eric Dolphy, who had already recorded on flute, alto sax, and bass clarinet, three of McIntyre's instruments. Dolphy may have helped McIntyre to a recording contract with Prestige.

"Freddie Hubbard said to me one night, 'Do you have your horn with you?' And I said, 'Well, it's in the car.' He said, 'Well, get it.' I was outside Minton's Playhouse. Eric was working there. He said, 'Well, bring your horn in. Eric will let you play.' So I brought my horn in, and Eric Dolphy said, 'Yeah, come on and play.' So we played some and shortly thereafter I heard from Prestige, because I had submitted a tape to them of some things that I had done in Boston with a group. The artist and repertory man in charge of the session, Desmond Edwards, said to me that he would like to do a couple of dates with me, but there was one stipulation. He wanted me to include Eric Dolphy on one of the dates. I had no problem with that, because Eric could play and he'd been very warm to me as a musician. I can't say that was true with other musicians that I had heard and been around at that particular time. It was unusual for someone to say, 'Yeah, come on and play' because of the insecurity of many musicians. Eric was a very secure person insofar as performance and playing his instruments. He wasn't threatened by anything."

New York musicians were usually less welcoming to strangers than was Dolphy—McIntyre talks about the "socialization" factor that kept him an outsider to the New York scene: "A young guy—a musician comes to town, and they want to know what you were into so they can deal with your personality. Were you into whiskey? Were you into pot? Were you into heroin? It was a 'high' culture and a musician that was into getting high could fit in many circles sooner than someone who was not." McIntyre was high on music, but that wasn't enough.

He recorded four albums in the early '60s, two for Prestige and two for United Artists. They did not change his life. He speaks of the reviews philosophically and with humor: "I've had some interesting reviews. They're all bad. I can remember the first album I ever put out—the one with Eric Dolphy—and what the reviewers said. The *down beat* reviewer starts out with 'Don't listen to this album if you have the slightest hint of a headache.' Then he goes on and he talks about our libidos. He calls us The Terrible Twins. Then he says, 'All in all, not a bad album. Two and a half stars.' So having been introduced in that light, I've been marking time—moving in other directions and developing myself."

Today *down beat*'s strictures on the McIntyre-Dolphy date *Looking Ahead* seem irrelevant. (Few records are good for headaches, although Norman Mailer once reported that listening to Sonny Rollins cured him of a migraine.) The album features five McIntyre compositions, including the lusty blues "Head Shakin'," as well as a relaxed version of Gershwin's "They All Laughed." Dolphy and McIntyre are nicely paired, Dolphy's dramatic entrances sounding as if he had wandered in off the street, while McIntyre's playing seems more centered. McIntyre intones "They All Laughed" like a straight man, but jeers and chortles on his own "Geo's Tune." On the waltz-like blues "Dianna," Dolphy interrupts McIntyre's loping flute solo with what becomes one of his wildest bass clarinet improvisations. The entire set, but especially its blues, sounds direct and often inspired today.

McIntyre's records did not sell, however, although some are collector's items today, and he faults the recording companies for not promoting him. The experience pushed him to trying to make a living as a performer. In 1961, after a traumatic evening in a Greenwich Village club, McIntyre quit. "The clubowner said, 'Well, we'll do a thing at the door and I'll split with you the receipts, depending on how many people come in.' I worked that night, and I came home to my wife. She said, 'How much money did you make?' I think I made a dollar. Maybe two dollars. I said to her, 'Well, baby, when I go back tomorrow night, it should be better.' My wife said, 'There'll be no tomorrow night.' At that particular moment I had two degrees in my pocket and I wanted to play, so I was willing to go back another night. I didn't go back and my wife said, wisely, 'Why don't you think about going into education?' I took some education courses and passed the examination in the New York public school system, and then I started teaching in October of 1961. So I understand the desire to play. I understand what it is and what it costs. Had I not opted to utilize my education I would have been going back there and prostituting myself."

McIntyre thinks it was important to walk away from degrading working conditions, although few musicians have done so willingly. "Musician" implies too specialized an idea. In the competitive music business a club owner can always replace a fractious musician with someone more pliable. Many musicians must have felt that the gesture of quitting an unpleasant job would be futile, and others have been happy to get any kind of gig playing the music they love. McIntyre points out that few musicians have trained themselves to do other things; he emulates the Africans who believe that a man can be many things at once, including a musician. "In traditional African systems, and I dare say in European systems prior to the twentieth century, it was possible for a person to be many things, because they had a 'man for all seasons' mentality—Leonardo da Vinci would do so many things. In our culture, a man tells himself, 'I'm a musician and so I'm only going to play my horn,' or 'I'm a composer, so I'm only going to compose.' A person in an African culture might be a musician, and he might be a painter, a dancer, and he might also be a chemist. Here they're saying, 'I can't take that kind of job, because that's beneath me. That would take me away from my music.' They become hung up with the notion of being a musician. Consequently, they work for little or nothing—at all costs—when in fact they could do more by doing something else and then making demands for better systems, better conditions under which to work."

By the time he retired McIntyre was being compared to both Ornette Coleman and Eric Dolphy, although his compositions were more complicated structurally than those of Coleman and his improvisations more traditionally lyrical than those of Dolphy. Most people don't hear very well: "One night Ornette and I were in the club called the Jazz Gallery, and Eric was playing and we came down after the set and were just sitting back, laughing and giggling and chewing the fat and it was very interesting because we were complimenting Dolphy and he was complimenting us. People that had heard Ornette or heard me thought that I was copying Ornette, but when Ornette came to Boston, people that heard Ornette were not surprised because they'd heard me. Ornette sounded different and I sounded different and Eric sounded different, and 'different' became a catch-all for everything."

From 1961 to 1967, McIntyre taught in the New York school systems; then for two years he was at Central State University in Wilberforce, Ohio, and then from 1969-71 at Wesleyan. Since 1971 he has been Director of the African-American Music and Dance concentration at the State University of New York at Old Westbury, having received a doctorate in education from the University of Massachusetts. He is also a Professor of Humanities. He teaches the history of the music and the history of African-Americans. "You cannot look at African-American music in the context of music in and of itself because it comes out of the social, political and economic phenomena that deal with black people. It's all related. You can't say, 'Well, let's forget that and look at the music.' It's impossible." He resists the "compartmentalization" of the music, the conventional distinctions about "styles." "Compartmentalization says that this is boogie-woogie, this is jazz, this is swing, this is bebop and so one sees those little compartments and thinks that they are entities unto themselves when in fact it's a continuum. And you may find an excellent performer that can run through the whole history before your ears."

While he "can't remember the last time I worked four weekends in a row," McIntyre has performed at Old Westbury and in New York. In 1970, the Bridgeport Symphony premiered his "Horizons," and he composed the score for an independent movie, *How Wide Is Sixth Avenue?* He took part in the 1976 sessions in

Sam Rivers's Studio Rivbea that were recorded by Douglas, and he has recorded five albums for the Danish label Steeplechase. One of them, *Introducing the Vibrations,* features McIntyre with a sextet (including four of McIntyre's former students). *Hindsight* and *Open Horizon* feature Kenny Drew, and *Home* is a set with the more raucous Jaki Byard. McIntyre records primarily his own compositions. In each record, he keeps the listener off balance and interested intellectually—*Home* opens with a piece that is 39 bars long; another contains 46, and most would challenge the mathematically inclined listener. "Amy" is a 12-bar blues, but played over what is usually called a calypso rhythm. (McIntyre is a stickler for proper terminology—he calls this rhythm the African Caribbean mode, as it appears in two continents and on several islands in between.) "Charlotte," the ballad on *Home,* is structurally complicated, but the simple, almost naive-sounding theme creates an impression of directness. McIntyre's compositions are oddly, but not synthetically, constructed. It was Ornette Coleman who spoke of letting musical phrases breathe. Why should every musical idea fit in four or eight measures? But Coleman allows for more freedom in the improvisational sections than does McIntyre; once he has composed a piece, McIntyre sticks to its scheme, and his musicians are expected to improvise within this structure. Not all of McIntyre's experiments succeed: it strikes me as somewhat perverse to perform "Body and Soul" on a bassoon over a calypso rhythm, but then McIntyre's is one of the few versions that will not be compared somehow to the Coleman Hawkins rendition.

At times, McIntyre seems as dedicated to keeping the listener as off balance in conversation as in his music. When I mentioned "Afro-American" music, I was instructed that "Afro" was a hair style, and that "African-American" is now proper. A drum set becomes, more accurately but cumbersomely, a "multiple percussion set." McIntyre has the sociologist's love of Latinate phraseology, but he also has an earthy side. He is a confident but not a cold man: many of his songs are meant to evoke members of his family— Eileen, Cousin Emma, Charlotte, Amy, his brother "Jawne," and sister "Puunti." In our conversation he was most enthusiastic when talking about his two sons and their prospects in college. He is complex and aggressive, but insightful. He notes that the popularity of "jazz" is accompanied by a growing tendency to call it "America's music." When it is most successful jazz is least likely to be tied in the public's mind to black culture. At times McIntyre seems contradictory: he stresses the continuum of African-American music but dislikes the word "jazz" because it identifies his music with the creations of relatively unskilled early practitioners of "jazz."

McIntyre is well prepared to continue teaching if the world is still not ready to hear him. But those people who do will experience a music that is rhythmically and structurally demanding and attractively varied. He writes in his notes to *Home* that African-American music is tied together by "feeling, rhythm, energy and creativity." His music is meant for those who want to "experience the past, present, and some of the future of music in the African-American tradition."

KARL BERGER

When German vibraphonist Karl Berger came to the United States in 1966, his immediate impact astonished his European friends. Critic Joachim Berendt's comments are excerpted on Berger's first ESP album: "Karl Berger's career is one of the most amazing I know of. In the mid-50s, he played an unspectacular jazz piano at the 'Cave' in Heidelberg, Germany, with boundless enthusiasm. He has been at it ever since, but nothing is left from the tame jazz excursions of those days. In the beginning of the '60s Berger went to Paris. Don Cherry had him join his international quintet and while one was still wondering about this fact, amazement began to spread about the development Berger had been going through from the old-time piano playing to the new, inspired vibraharp playing. Cherry took Berger along to the USA, and today the Heidelberg-born vibist is the most sought-after man on his instrument within the New York avant-garde. The musicians are saying unhesitatingly that he is the world's best new vibraharp player."

The vibraharp or vibraphone, a metal-keyed adaptation of a xylophone with an electrically produced tremolo, seemed an unlikely instrument for the jazz avant-garde: previously Lionel Hampton helped it swing, Red Norvo made it thump and Milt Jackson forced it to play a mellow blues. But it also had been used for countless syrupy ballad performances that exploited the instrument's gentle pulse and ceaseless tremolo. (Technically an alteration of volume rather than a variation in pitch, like vibrato, the tremolo has much of the latter's effect.) Berger took the motor out of his instrument and offered a brittle sound that cuts through the most lively ensemble. Still, Berendt's amazement was not with the instrument, but with Berger's playing. His surprise would be more understandable if one had heard Berger's more tame performances, but by the time Berger was in the United States his new style had arrived too—his astringent sound and technical facility proved attractive to a variety of New York musicians, as did his scholarly musicianship and experience with the classical avant-garde. Musicians realized that his "rather tame" piano playing could add a firm harmonic or rhythmic foundation to a performance that needed either, and yet his vibraphone playing is often frenetic and harmonically dramatic, his phrases short bursts or long, arching swoops. Berger is intrigued by Balinese music—and some of his improvisations have the charming simplicity, repetition and rhythmic variety of that nation's gamelan.

Berger had entered a Paris inhabited by many American musicians—Cherry and Anthony Braxton among them—who were investigating contemporary music of all sorts. They were playing in a foreign country because they were ignored at home. Most were eager to view their creations as part of a world music, and some, like Cherry, talked of a world *folk* music to which "jazz" could be adapted. Berger was a natural to help break down barriers—in 1963 he would earn a Ph.D. in musicology and sociology from the University of Heidelberg, and he knew everything in Ornette Coleman's repertoire. He was heard on Don Cherry's *Symphony for Improvisers* and *Eternal Rhythm*, the latter a recording that Berger helped organize and that exploits Balinese rhythms and musical ideas. Since the mid-60s, Berger has recorded for ESP, Milestone,

Karl Berger and Ed Blackwell *by Michael Ullman*

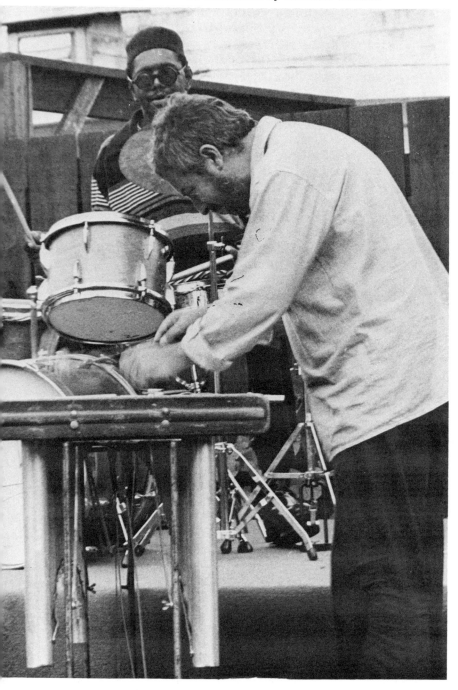

Horo, Free Music Production and other labels, including an album with the group Musica Ellectronica Viva: it features three musicians rooted in jazz—saxophonist Steve Lacy, trombonist Garrett List and Berger—as well as three musicians trained in contemporary "classical" styles—composer-pianist Frederic Rzewski, Richard Teitelbaum (a synthesist who has recorded with Anthony Braxton) and Alvin Curran.

In 1971 Berger and Ornette Coleman started the Creative Music Studio. It has thrived. Originally in New York City, the Studio moved to Woodstock, New York, where Berger has leased an outmoded resort called Oehler's. (Oehler was a German who may never have adequately adapted to this country's habits: at his resort he installed a now popular swimming pool, and a lovely soccer field, which remains unused. People at the Studio still talk of "Oehlerisms," such as the sign rigidly defining the uncomfortable consequences of being late for breakfast. "Caution: Men's Room" could have been an Oehlerism. Students still reside in Oehler's cottages: the Chateau, the Lorraine, the Roma, the Astoria and the Honeymoon. Concerts are given in the Champagne Room, meant to suggest Lawrence Welk.) The Studio is dedicated to providing basic training for musicians so that they may subsequently be able to perform in all contemporary traditions. Berger himself seems readily able to reconcile opposites: trained in Heidelberg conservatories, he is most happy performing informally in outdoor settings. He is a rotund, dark-haired man who laughs, or rather giggles, suddenly and attractively. When I saw him he was dressed in sandals, jeans and a baggy shirt, yet his philosophy is serious and he stresses the importance of self-discipline. His students receive extensive training in tuning and rhythms, and they can study such topics as "How different countries relate to nature in their music." All the practice and discipline should lead, Berger says, to the point where we "become instruments—when the music can flow through freely, like electricity through a transmitter."

I talked to Berger after a benefit concert for drummer

Ed Blackwell; in the near background, on the grassy hill overlooking the main building of the Studio, five or six students were playing a variety of percussion instruments. Berger looked at me a little wistfully and spoke of his plans to build a "room of silence" where one could meditate. All music, he said through the din, must come from the background of silence.

Berger was born in 1935. "I was ten years old when the war was over, and then I spent most of the time until I was twenty in my hometown Heidelberg. I studied there at the conservatory, starting at the age of twelve or so. We were American territory in Heidelberg—it was the American headquarters. Consequently, the Americans opened up all kinds of clubs and boys' centers, similar to the youth clubs around here. In my club they taught kids how to improvise and play the Shearing type of music. I played in dance bands before I got out of school." Exposed to jazz, Berger started to play in a small club in Heidelberg: "In 1954 a club opened that was dedicated to jazz—it was a student club of some sort. At that time a lot of American musicians were in the various Army bands in the area—in Stuttgart, Frankfurt, Mannheim, none of them further away than seventy or eighty miles. All these musicians would come to this club to play. There were a lot of people who later got famous on the scene: Don Ellis, Cedar Walton and Leo Wright. I had an opportunity to play with all these people almost every night. I quit my conservatory studies at that time."

Berger was exclusively a pianist until 1960, when he took up the vibraphone. "I started traveling, playing in other places and everywhere we came the pianos were bad. I just wanted to have an instrument that I would know what it would sound like. Then we went on a tour with a French vibraphone player, Michel Hausser. He was the top vibraphone player in France, and I played in his band for a tour of Germany. Then I visited him and played with him in Paris. I went to Paris for the first time at the end of 1960. He had this instrument I'm still playing now. He had that built for himself and just gave it back to the factory. I said, 'Well, listen, I'll buy it back from the factory'." Berger had the instrument modified to produce the exact sound he wanted, and later he himself took out the electrical devices that create an artificial tremolo. "That motor gives you a certain vibrato effect, but it also disturbs the natural vibrato that comes from the metal. The solution that most vibraphone players choose is to keep it in there but not have it going all the time. It's probably a good solution, except that the stuff that's in between the resonators and the keys stops the sound from really getting out its special qualities." Berger's instrument has a sharp quality unique to his playing—machinery like that he removed muffles the highest frequencies of the metal's vibrations. "The instruments are built according to what school is really prevalent at the time. Most of the vibraphones were built to get the sound that, let's say, Milt Jackson and later Gary Burton were trying to get. Milt Jackson was looking for a real clean sound, but he also wanted the middle ranges to be really mellow. Gary Burton is interested only in technique—he doesn't care about what sound he gets. Metal is a very sensitive thing. It really needs a lot of fine tuning. My instrument was done by one person by ear. Today companies cut them with machines and they put them together and they're never in tune. Because the tuning system that we hear doesn't work exactly like the machines do."

In 1963 Berger received a doctorate from the University of Heidelberg. "I went to the university studying musicology and sociology; you cannot study just music at the university in Europe. I wrote a thesis on the definition of the function of music in the Soviet system between 1948 and '58, which was between Stalin and Khrushchev—and with the example of Shostakovitch. I studied what was officially determined about how music would play a role in the party organization and in the ideological development of the Soviet system." Since this was before the Wall was built Berger was able to find in East Berlin the necessary Russian documents translated into German.

In the mid-60s Berger moved to Paris, where he

immediately met Don Cherry. "I met Don in Paris in 1965, in March. I moved to Paris from Germany and we met the same evening. It was incredible. From then on I played with Don for about a year and a half. I knew most of the tunes Don was trying to play because he played a lot of Ornette's material which was on the records, and he played a lot of standard material: Charlie Parker, Thelonious Monk tunes, and so on, exactly the type of mixture we were playing before I met him. But then we learned all these new tunes that he had written himself, or Ornette pieces that were not published—things like that. Actually we had no trouble fitting together right away." Berger had unwittingly prepared for this meeting by studying Ornette Coleman's music: "From the beginning, when Ornette's music was coming on the scene, I picked up everything I could, because that sounded exactly like some of the things I had in mind, about how composition, improvisation should be to me. It was like I felt like I was part of that school in a way. With Don Cherry I had this chance to have a close communication with them."

Berger's wife, who sings under the name Ing Rid, was about to have their first baby when Cherry went to New York to record *Complete Communion* with Gato Barbieri. Berger stayed home. "I played with Steve Lacy for that month in that same club in Paris." Lacy was on a Monk kick at the time—he recorded a whole album of Monk tunes with Don Cherry. "We also played only Monk tunes. But I'm certain that that's the last month ever that Steve played only Monk tunes, because we took those pieces apart."

Berger followed Cherry to New York in the fall of 1966. There they played a Town Hall concert and did some nights at the Five Spot. They also recorded *Symphony for Improvisers*. Although he had been working steadily in Europe Berger felt that being in New York he could further his music. "The European scene is very alive in ways of presentations, but I had several things in mind that I wanted to try and do and I just couldn't find the musicians to do it in Europe. The scene is much more defined and categorized in Europe than here. If you're a jazz player, you're a jazz player. If you're an avant-garde player, you're an avant-garde player. And there's serious music. There's all these categories and it's hard to bridge the gaps. They are established in the radio stations which are organized and almost government run. If you don't fit one of their categories you're in trouble. In the U.S., there was nothing happening in a way. There were all these musicians, but not much work." For immigration reasons, Berger continued to spend time in Europe, but he was here to stay.

"I was extremely lucky actually. I rehearsed with a lot of groups like Roswell Rudd's group, Marion Brown's group—always rehearsal situations. No money. And I worked with the drummer Horacee Arnold. He formed a group that played in schools." This group, funded by "Young Audiences," contained at various times Reggie Workman, Vishnu Wood and Sam Rivers. The experience was important to Berger, proving that this new music was accessible at least to children and providing the impetus for his educational projects: "I saw that, quite contrary to our previous experience, there were a lot of people who could like the music at an early age. They were eleven or twelve years old. We played mostly for sixth graders. There was just so much enthusiasm about the music that it was hard for me to believe that there wouldn't be many people ready to open up to more creative aspects of music than they usually do. I realized that the problem was educational, and I decided that this education should come from the artist first-hand. So the first thing I did was to write to the New School for Social Research with a proposal for introducing an improvisation course. I taught there two years before I started the Studio. In 1971 we formed a foundation, the Creative Music Foundation. Ornette Coleman was a co-founder. Ornette was probably the one musician in New York who always supported whatever I was trying to do all the way and always encouraged me. He would always find time. I considered myself for a long time a student of Ornette's. He's an incredibly giving personality."

Berger soon moved the Studio to Woodstock; its first full-time session there was in 1973. Berger thinks it was important to get away from the city. "Teaching at the New School, I realized that the city environment would not be conducive to ongoing study. There's too much distraction. And there's always a certain kind of noise level. You cannot eliminate it. If you want to study music, you have to start from silence. I'm interested in working in a natural environment—if you learn to play outdoors, no environment will give you trouble."

A student's day in the regular Woodstock sessions begins at nine o'clock with what Berger calls "wake-up procedures": "body awareness practices, gymnastics or exercises that derive from various traditions such as Tai Chi or Yoga. I think that to be a good player you should be in control of your body as much as possible. I'm also personally very interested in the relationship of music and dance, as are quite a few of the students. Then at ten o'clock the people do what we call basic practice: timing and tuning practices without instruments. We are trying to stabilize people's feel for rhythm at first. I developed a sort of system which we call Gamela/Taki, whereby we divide all possible meters from 3 to 27 into odd and even counts, Gamela being odd and Taki being even. [In other words, to give the rhythm of a waltz, one only has to repeat 'Gamela.' To recreate 2/4 time, one says 'Taki.' All other rhythms can be seen as multiples or combinations of these numbers.] So we recite them, practicing certain meters by calling out those words rather than counting. We practice those numbers and then we make up melodies to fit the cycles. So we begin unconsciously to do very unusual cycles—say 13, or 9. We just practice these for an hour straight, not using instruments, vocalizing the rhythms and playing them with our hands. And I've found that every time a session starts, after two weeks of doing that everybody's timing has improved 100 percent. It's amazing." Another discovery is that one's tuning improves with one's rhythmic sense: "Tuning is actually nothing else but understanding time. Because it's vibration too. In the same period we do actual tuning practices where, let's say, one note is held against every conceivable chord combination, so that you understand the overtone qualities. So an 'A' has a thousand different tunings, depending on what chord situation it is. Then from 11:30 to 1:00 people are busy in what we call applied theory: ear training, sight reading, interval training, chords and chord progressions. We try to have various groups: intermediate, advanced and beginning. In the afternoons from 2:00 to 6:00 we do merely conceptual work. It means the guiding artists come up and work on their own concepts and pieces, orchestral works, and they actually work toward a performance with the students." Berger's catalog lists thirty-two musicians who have served as guiding artists, usually creating large orchestral works with the students. The artists include Sam Rivers, George Russell, Roscoe Mitchell and also John Cage and Richard Teitelbaum. The list is weighted heavily toward those who are playing on what Rivers calls the "frontiers" of music, but it also includes such brilliant older musicians as Lee Konitz and Steve Lacy.

The Studio is still developing: students must submit a tape or audition to be accepted, and musicians come from Europe and Japan as well as the United States. More and more the concerts at Woodstock feature pieces composed by, as well as performed by, the students. Berger hopes to develop something of a club atmosphere in the Champagne Room: that means adding a little soundproofing, and, one would hope, a change of name. He wants to present student concerts on Friday nights and professional performances on Saturdays. He encourages other arts too: at the student concert I attended one young man read from a journal, and a dancer accompanied some of the music. I asked Berger what he expected his students to do when they left the Studio, and he seemed surprised: "Oh, we are not really career-oriented here. Not at all. The students that come here understand before they come that what they are coming for is to expand their knowledge, to expand their creative capacity. What careers they're following is a whole other ball game. So we are not training anybody for any kind of career at all. It's not like the Berklee School where you can join a band or you can work in studios. Usually we get people who have already gone through that type of program and are interested in what they can do as composers or as improvisers."

Although few of his records remain in the catalogs, Berger has not neglected his recording career. The titles of his compositions reflect his basic concerns: his ESP recording includes "Scales" and "Steps"; his FMP recording "Tuning/Timing"; and his Milestone work, "Tune In," "With Silence" and "Clarity." Clarity is a recurrent theme in his conversation and a goal in his music-making. Clarity and precision, but also wit and inventiveness or, what one critic has called Berger's "crisp irony," are integral to his style. He is consciously eclectic. In the liner notes to a recent record, Berger suggests: "Now there are as many traditions as there are people," and he invites us to "tune in." This is "live time," he asserts, and he wants us to feel it with him.

RAN BLAKE

Ran Blake lives several blocks to the west of
Boston's Symphony Hall and works less than a block
to its south. He is a pianist who has composed pieces
honoring Susan Sontag, Fritz Lang, Leroi Jones, Edith
Piaf, Steve Biko and black evangelist Sister Tee, "a
woman on 124th Street with an enormous Bible—with a
small bottle of gin inside—and if she had to use that to
convert you she would." He is a white man in his forties
who plays convincing gospel piano, and whose
earliest musical influences included Bartok and the
music of The Church of God in Christ in Hartford,
Connecticut, where he used to "sanctify and protest."
Blake convinced the president of Bard College to allow
him to construct a major in jazz: Blake graduated in
1960 only to discover that what he was playing was not
jazz. He was then, he told me, "a fish on a land garden,"
improvising Bartok-like jazz pieces but unable to play
convincingly with a rhythm section and unwilling to
notate his "classical" compositions. He believed that
he had to be either a jazz musician or a classicist.
Fortunately Gunther Schuller was then publicizing
what he called "Third Stream" music, designed to
integrate the classical and jazz traditions. The concept
resulted in a lot of what Blake calls "Stan Kenton
Hollywood type music," but for Ran Blake "Third
Stream" was a godsend. As a musician, he could swim

in the stream between the islands of jazz and classical music. In private lessons Gunther Schuller gave Blake the confidence he needed: "The main thing was I had no identity. I didn't know who I was. Gunther was able to get me to respect myself, although he didn't give me a bouquet of roses. All my early experiences—with Mahalia Jackson, jazz, Bartok—were dynamite, but they never blended together till Gunther." Today Ran Blake is the head of the Third Stream Department of The New England Conservatory of Music. In the past several years he has made nine albums, and he is astonished to observe that his music is developing in a "jazz" direction. Dedicated as Blake is to his own performances, he is just as interested in finding young musicians—different from their fellows—who might use the Third Stream Department to find themselves musically. He teaches six days a week, hoping "to get my students into their own music."

Blake has been picking out melodies on the piano since he was three or four. He has always had curiosity; although he has had many teachers and a lot of lessons, he is largely self-taught, and he has a discipline for himself as stringent as any that could have been imposed on him. He grew up in Connecticut and in Springfield, Massachusetts, and was, as he told me, "very unhappy at a little school in Suffield, Connecticut." As a result, he used to go home—while others were involved in sports—to "play the piano by the hour, although not in a disciplined, conservatory, Czerny way. I probably did exercises for all of ten minutes." After those exercises, he would become programmatic, trying to tell "stories with strange chords." His childhood was spent "playing fantasy and dream worlds." He was self-involved and isolated, hearing only classical records. "Then I studied with a wonderful pianist, Ray Cassarino, who had just come off the road with Woody Herman. Ray encouraged me to start really hearing records. Until he came along no one said, 'why not hear records?' So at age thirteen and fourteen, hearing Bartok and Debussy, I felt I was stupid because I didn't read music and I was going into

Ran Blake *by Randy Matusow*

music by the back door." Cassarino not only taught the young pianist the basic chords and intervals, but just as important, he encouraged Blake to investigate on his own. The techniques the boy discovered were those appropriate to his own music.

Blake listened seriously to contemporary classical music before jazz, and to film music before classical. "The very tip" or beginning of his involvement in music resulted from his interest in movies. (Blake still tries to see seven movies a month, and attends virtually every major New York film festival.) "I listened spellbound to the mystery music in films, but you had to sit through all the rhapsodic lovemaking and banality." He bought soundtrack recordings, including *A Streetcar Named Desire* and *Destination Moon*. "Victor Young's *Samson and Delilah* lasted me just one hour one afternoon: then I threw the record away. But the more strange soundtracks led me to Prokofiev and Debussy." His standard for judging these European pieces was derived from African-American music: "The film music was like a weak Mexican meal, so I kept getting more and more hungry. I came to Bartok as late as sixteen and seventeen, and with Debussy, it was *Afternoon of a Faun*. I couldn't stand the *Clair de Lune*s and the Ravel *Boleros*. As soon as it got too hummable or whistleable or predictable I got bored. There wasn't that added beat that suddenly Mahalia [Jackson] would add in her music or Sweet Georgia Peach. Whereas the *Rite of Spring* always could leave you panting for more." The Bartok that interested Blake included the *Music for Strings, Celeste and Percussion* and the *Sonata for Two Pianos and Percussion*. Typically he disliked the *Concerto for Orchestra* because it was "too happy."

Although Blake's parents wanted him to go to Williams, he entered Bard College in 1956. He negotiated a deal with President James Case that allowed him to learn in New York City from prominent jazz musicians, including Oscar Peterson and Thelonious Monk. Blake's conversations with Monk about music occurred at a bar, but he studied in a more conventional way with Peterson. Blake had approximately eleven lessons with Peterson, whose fluent and sometimes glib-sounding pianistics seem antithetical to Blake's own style. Nevertheless Blake always cites Peterson's influence: "I was so into jagged things. Oscar did so much to loosen things up and to get me to have different feelings. I took notes at the lessons and years later I worked on this flow of things, sitting and relaxing. I know I gained a lot of things, including softness in tone. He did stress making me play jazz. And I think that it helped me to try to play jazz, even if I felt then I was mediocre. Staying in tempo, not merely indulging myself in little fantasy things, helped my other music."

To Blake, jazz meant rhythmical excitement and a hornlike line in his right hand. When he graduated from Bard College, Blake realized that he was not strictly playing jazz. "I couldn't expect to be an Art Tatum in technique or a Monk in originality. But why was I better when doing quasi-Bartok things? They were more successful than my jazz pieces, which didn't swing. I didn't make it with trios. I could do a little better in blues and gospel, but I really didn't make it. Yet once in a while I'd do a ballad by myself and people would say, 'That's interesting, Ran. You're not just a total schmuck.' "

He worked for Atlantic Records one winter, ransacking the tape library for unreleased sessions of Ray Charles and Thelonious Monk. Blake first met Gunther Schuller while working as a guard for the Newport Jazz Festival; he got the job because he recognized people like Dizzy Gillespie. Blake remembers that throughout his week in Newport he kept a bottle of Seven-Up close by; he knew that Erroll Garner loved Seven-Up and was hoping for a chance to offer the bottle to Garner. Instead Blake got to ask for Schuller's autograph.

Blake spent several of his college summers at Lenox, Massachusetts, where Schuller and John Lewis had opened the Lenox School of Jazz. There as in New York he was encouraged by some musicians and ignored by others. "People put me down in New York, but there were some very supportive, wonderful black musicians. Kenny Dorham said he wouldn't hire me in a group, but he said he would love to hire me opposite him if he had a week in the Vanguard. I said, 'Well, why not admit I'm not going to make it?' He said, 'No, you have something very special but I just don't think it blends with us.' I realized that with some very important exceptions it was still the black music that I liked the best in jazz. I was mad about Chris Connor, some Russo things for Kenton, but that kind of thing that Miles was doing, and Mingus, and Roach and George Russell—well, I didn't fit in, so what the hell was I? Now of course, with Braxton and what Karl Berger's doing, it's not so rigid, but in '58 and '59, there was still Bud Powell. You had to do one thing or the other."

At least that was the way it seemed until one day at Lenox when John Lewis took Blake over to meet Gunther Schuller again. Blake was working on the piece that would become "Silver Fox," and Schuller helped Blake edit his composition, separating "the wheat from the chaff." He forced Blake to listen to himself more carefully. "In my music at the time there were probably some very beautiful, primitive melodies; there were some sounds from field cries, there was third-rate Copland, and probably some serial soap opera music from afternoon NBC. The cliches would abound, and then there might be a beautiful passage and then it would be terrible again. If I had written a piece on paper, there might have been one twenty-second phrase that was personal and the rest cliches. He'd play me the cliches and where I got the things from. I think Gunther's editing made me very scrupulous, maybe too scrupulous at times. If I have a record, if there's one little weak scrap, I'd rather leave it in now, because that's the truth. I played it at that moment. Now I don't want to cut, cut, cut."

After graduating from Bard, Blake moved to New York City and continued to study with Schuller, whom he saw irregularly between 1960 and 1964. Blake notes that Schuller's Manhattan apartment was "the place to go in New York. I'd be there for five hours, but there might be only an hour and a half of lesson. The phone rang. Someone like Coltrane would drop by." Schuller was able to focus Blake's interests, to give him confidence and at the same time make him more self-critical. According to Blake, Schuller has been "lauded for many unique abilities, but perhaps the most unusual one is his imagination and compassion for the street musician and his uncanny ability to discover the hidden gifts in people before they do themselves."

It wasn't long before Blake began recording. His first session was a stunning recital with the black singer Jeanne Lee, one of the most important singers associated with the avant-garde. She has abandoned words now, but on that session she recorded "Sometimes I Feel Like a Motherless Child" in an arrangement that recalls that of the folk singer Odetta, and "Evil Blues," an almost corny blues popularized by Josh White. The record begins with a version of "Laura," about which Gunther Schuller has written: "'Laura' is the ideal vehicle for a Lee-Blake collaboration. Their extraordinary ears and their sensitivity allow them considerable latitude to search out the deepest harmonic nooks and crannies of this standard tune; yet they always return to tonal home base— though in ways that can easily baffle the ordinary musician or listener. Here the many worlds of music— Schoenbergian atonality, Billie Holiday's sadly poignant laments, the American popular ballad, extemporization, and composition—all intertwine." Yet the music seems more direct than this suggests. Lee's voice is warm, her interpretations daring but focused and emotional: they owe as much to Abbey Lincoln as to Billie Holiday, but there is no reason to think of her work as derivative. Blake's accompaniment is often bleak and dissonant: he takes the tunes out of tempo and revamps their harmonies. Remarkably, neither Lee nor her partner betrays any insecurity. Their version of "Where the Flamingos Fly" dignifies a sentimental though unusual story. This astringent tale of a woman's lover who has been deported is followed by a sprightly call to an erotic vacation, "Season in the Sun." In the first chorus of "Summertime" Lee flattens the too familiar solo while Blake's right hand wanders casually over the piano; he introduces the second chorus with some surprisingly emphatic chords. Everything in this version is unexpected and fresh, even down to the last bars when Lee's voice seems to shrink suddenly—she sounds as vulnerable as the baby she is reassuring. The record, now out of print, is notable also for the Blake solo "gospel" number, "Church on Russell Street."

In 1965, Blake recorded a solo album for the small New York label ESP. Blake lauds Schuller's taste in musicians; Blake's taste in compositions is equally praiseworthy. His concerts include artfully chosen jazz classics, from "Green Dolphin Street" to McCoy Tyner's "Search for Peace." The ESP album includes "There'll Be Some Changes Made," a tune that ends rather too abruptly, George Russell's "Stratusphunk," Ornette Coleman's "Lonely Woman," "Good Morning Heartache," as well as some of Blake's own compositions. "Sister Tee" is his gospel piece; it seems designed to evoke several kinds of gospel music, opening out of tempo with a repeated downward run punctuated by trills in the right hand: this is followed by half a chorus of some stomping two-handed music, which is interrupted by the fragmented opening repeated. The piece continues, alternating sweet harmonies and rousing rhythms with cold dissonances that fill up empty spaces. It is pleasing and exciting, but suggests a comment Blake made jokingly to me: "I get nervous if I stay in one key more than a minute." He seems to get uneasy if he stays in one rhythm that long too. Blake's gospel playing owes an acknowledged debt to the long-time accompanist of Mahalia Jackson, Mildred Falls, whose heavy beat and dancing triplet figures, often voiced in fourths, are echoed in Blake's versions of "Just a Closer Walk With Thee."

Blake's next record, *Blue Potato and Other Outrages*, was his last for seven years. Issued in 1969, *Blue Potato* reflects Blake's social concerns. It is a record that seems self-consciously avant-garde: Marian McPartland told me emphatically that it was too far out for her, while Blake himself suggests it is not a jazz album: "I don't think it can be judged that way. It does not have the certain kind of excitement that McCoy Tyner has and Horace Silver, and yet I don't think it's 100 percent trash. You might like *Blue Potato*, but really to hear the whole record through, unless you've heard a lot of Satie that day—I just think you might fall asleep. In the most successful pieces—one is 'Malcolm X'—there might be a black gut feeling, but it's certainly not black music." *Blue Potato* is an (uncomplimentary) name for the police, while "Malcolm X" is the third part of a suite called "Three Seeds"; it follows evocations of Regis Debray and Che Guevara. As Blake told Len Lyons, "I can't limit myself to writing about a guy touching a woman, or bluesville Kansas City, or how to smoke a joint." He is not going to play classic blues, but neither is he going merely to indulge in fantasies like those he created in childhood—his music, Blake seems to say, is socially useful. His compositions recreate the world he perceives, expressing his attitudes towards human events. To the trivial tin pan alley sound of "Chicago" he adds dissonance and some resounding thumps. We are meant to think of riots and racism. But there are a limited number of ways in which to express outrage on the piano, and even someone as committed as Blake finds it difficult to differentiate musically his distress at Mayor Daley's antics and his anger at the atrocities of the Greek colonels. At a recent performance, Blake introduced Billy Strayhorn's world-weary ballad, "Lush Life." It's an antiromantic tale of disappointed love; sodden, grey faces and dimly lit bars. Blake gives it his own plot: "There's an elderly Jewish lady living in a rather dark house. When she's lonely, she goes up into her attic where she looks through her old pictures and things. While there, she trips over a music box and it plays a tune that gives her faith and brings her back into the present time." The plot has more to do with Blake's pianistics than with Strayhorn's idea of the song. Blake's story allows him to indulge in one of his long, bleak introductions and to state the theme, when it comes, in a typically brittle style, high in the treble; it has a tinkly sound appropriate to the music box, but not perhaps to an unhappy lover.

When Gunther Schuller became the President of The New England Conservatory of Music in 1967, he took Ran Blake to Boston with him. At first Blake worked on a variety of projects, from teaching improvisation to acting as co-director of the Conservatory's community service projects. In 1973 he was made the Chairperson of the Third Stream Department. In a lecture he defined his type of Third Stream as "an improvised synthesis of ethnic cabaret or Afro-American music with what has been called for the last few years European avant-garde." Since then he has expanded his ideas to include any two strands of contemporary music. Blake urges his students to investigate ethnic music—he himself performs Greek music ("Never on Sunday," "Vradiaziana"), Italian folk music ("Bella Ciao") as well as jazz classics. Although the department is small (Blake would like it to have thirty to forty students), it has attracted people from Europe, Asia and South America. He does this by concentrating on ear training. In the first year, students are provided with a variety of taped music. They learn to listen and memorize. Students might be asked to learn the melody line of a Billie Holiday performance, and then to memorize the bass line. In the second year students expand their knowledge of musical styles and develop their own improvisational skills. The last two years are devoted to helping them develop performance skills as well as their own "personal roots."

Blake works almost constantly: I attended a Saturday afternoon session of a seminar designed to expose students to different musics. The subject of the day was the blues, and several of the students made presentations. One explained the blues harmonica, another played a tape of his tenor sax performance of Coltrane's "Bessie's Blues." He interspersed choruses of his own improvisations with Coltrane's licks: the game was to figure out which were his own choruses. When Blake isn't teaching, he's recruiting—a small program like his is always endangered by the economic problems that plague all schools.

After class, Blake and I walked to his office, and he told me about the problems of maintaining the triple life of an administrator, teacher and creative musician. He wants to revive the aural tradition of music teaching, but also would like to maintain a minimal social life. As he searched for a slip of paper with an important phone number, he told me that teaching was his first priority but that he is pleased with the recent progress of his performing career. He is also interested in the direction his music has been taking. I mentioned to him that he is something of an anomaly still among improvising musicians: while jazz solos tend to get longer and longer, Blake's music is remarkable for its brevity. *Breakthru*, a solo album recorded in 1975, has fourteen performances; the longest is under five minutes, while four others take less than two. Blake attributes his conciseness to his listening habits and to his tendency to edit himself: "I spent three summers with Billie Holiday's records just falling in love, making love to six albums for a ten-week period. That structure—the 32-bar form on the 78 record—I respect. What Armstrong could do in a minute and a half. I don't like a lot of long things. It bothers me about a lot of free music today: there is nothing more exciting than hearing somebody scream in the middle of the piece for two minutes. But if it goes for a whole side of a record it does not interest me as much."

In a lecture, Blake suggested another reason for this brevity: "In Third Stream music improvisation, the performer must pay a considerable amount of attention to structure because quite often there is an absence of an overt rhythm, an element of music that acts as an important cohesive force and one that often has 'saved' much music (weak in other areas). This attention calls for a high consciousness level in emphasizing compositional devices. However, too much conscious abstract form can rob the music of its blood and its surprise. The best remedy—brevity." Recently Blake has been allowing more overt rhythms into his music, and he has recorded with such unabashed jazz players as Ricky Ford, a young tenor player from Boston whom Blake discovered when Ford was only sixteen. Not surprisingly, as Blake's performances become more rhythmical they tend to be longer. He is, perhaps, developing more of the Oscar Peterson flow.

Blake is modest, dedicated and self-critical, often excessively so: he will talk about the one or two decent pieces on one of his records, and I've heard him suggest to an audience that they probably won't like the next piece. He bursts with ideas in conversation; when he's excited each sentence swallows the tail of its predecessor. But on stage Blake is marvelously controlled and introspective. Each of his concerts in the Boston area draws a large crowd of his friends, students and colleagues. At a club called Lulu White's in Boston's South End, I heard him play a set that included tunes by Cole Porter, Ellington, Monk and Mal Waldron, a piece by Milton Nascimento, an Italian folk song, and six Catalonian songs. He announced at the end of the set that it had been "one of the most joyful sets I've done, so I'd like to do something more typical." He then played his tribute to the murdered South African Steve Biko, as if to suggest that music is not all fun.

Blake's piano style has been called pianistic rather than "hornlike." He is attentive to the sound of the piano and eager to exploit its possibilities. One of his pieces begins before we hear anything: Blake depresses silently several keys so the first notes he hits will set up the overtones he desires. His playing is typically percussive and often dissonant, but he is concerned with dynamics and he varies his attacks. Often he answers resounding chords with a delicate treble trill. He plays familiar songs, but he will fragment, isolate, or disguise the melody. As he told Len Lyons, he is still experimenting with techniques. "But I really think there are a lot of sounds on the grand piano that I haven't gotten to yet, like horn sounds, very percussive sounds, sounds like a woodwind section, overlapping sounds you can get into by hitting the instrument, caressing the upper register, or pursuing degrees of touch and accent."

If Blake has been performing more in the past years, he has not given up his other responsibilities. He writes occasional musical criticism for *The Bay State Banner*, a black-owned newspaper published in the Boston area, and he talks about becoming more active in the community. He has playfully described his own brand of Third Stream music as having a "generous allowance of European dissonance with ethnic gut topped off by a dash of a highly developed form of fantasy." Blake's "fantasies" are important to us today because he has disciplined himself, because he has listened critically and imaginatively to his own work and to that of others. He has the qualities he encourages in his students—"good ears, imagination, a strong non-pompous ego, sense of his self-portrait, and a tolerant interest in other people and twentieth century cross-currents."

RAY MANTILLA

Latin percussionist Ray Mantilla is a good-looking, light-skinned man with a smooth boyish face and dark hair; he looks considerably younger than he is, although because of all the years spent "fighting the street out there," he was surprised when I told him so. Born in 1934 in a largely Puerto Rican section of the Bronx, Mantilla has been an almost anonymous member of numerous Latin bands, but he has also played and recorded with such jazz stars as Herbie Mann, Max Roach, Charlie Mingus, Freddie Hubbard, Gato Barbieri, Sonny Stitt, Joe Farrell and Larry Coryell. He has worked at Newport Festivals, in clubs, and at a Brooklyn Philharmonic concert. With composer David Amram, he performed at the Mariposa, Philadelphia, and Owen Sound folk festivals. He toured Europe with Max Roach, South America with Herbie Mann, Japan with Art Blakey, and in 1977 he went to Cuba with the first group of American musicians to visit there since the advent of the Castro regime.

For years Mantilla has been trying to escape the "box" in which traditional bands restrict their percussionists. He is an energetic and ambitious man who sees his life as a slow battle to achieve recognition and the freedom to play as he wants. His measured progress has been marred by setbacks as trivial as a gall bladder infection on the day of an important recording date and as all-encompassing as a long bout with drug addiction. He is currently working steadily, but even now is edgy about success. Superstitious, he notes that whenever his career is progressing smoothly, something comes along "that knocks me on my ass." In April 1978, Mantilla recorded his first album as a leader, benefiting from the public's acceptance of various kinds of "fusion" music. Equally adept at Puerto Rican and Cuban rhythms, Mantilla is refining his skills in Brazilian styles and in jazz. "Talk about fusion," he says. "Everybody says cross over, fusion and all that. I'm the real fusion."

Mantilla did not play the congas until he was eighteen and out of high school, but he grew up in an area rich in Latin musicians: "I lived at 135th Street on the West Side. When I got a little older, about nine or ten, we moved uptown towards Prospect Avenue, 149th Street and Southern Boulevard. That's where Eddie Palmieri came from; Tito Puente lived around there. All the big name guys in salsa today. Ray Barretto lived on Prospect Avenue. I lived in that area where everybody would take up the drum—like the congas. That's what I wanted to do and I just worked at it, worked at it, kept working at it. After high school, there was nothing really to do that I liked much. That's one way to get out of the streets. I just kept playing the drum and one thing led to another."

His parents separated when Mantilla was eight, but before his father returned to his native Peru, Mantilla heard him play acoustic guitar. The elder Mantilla was an educated man, an electrical engineer who helped design the wiring at Fordham University. Mantilla has eight Peruvian brothers as a result of his father's rather irregular married life: "When he came over here, he already had two children. He came over here, married my mother, and I was the only kid and he went back and he lived in Peru for twenty years. He got married over there, had more kids." His brothers, he adds, are diligently working to help publicize Mantilla's music in Latin America. The family of Mantilla's

Ray Mantilla *courtesy Inner City Records*

mother was earthier: "They're all farmers: Puerto Ricans from the land. What could they make it in? A great grocery store that made a lot of money? On my father's side everybody's got to have a degree. Me—I was caught in the middle of all this because he split when I was eight—I had to do all this by myself. I went to school—you know kids, the school, and the systems over here. Everybody was too busy doing music and having a ball. At that time everybody was a dance freak and that's when the big dances were happening. Machito was coming up and Tito Rodriguez was just coming up and Tito Puente. Charlie Parker was out there. It was a melting pot."

Mantilla had a large record collection and he loved to dance at the Palladium, "the starting place for all the Latin bands." He got through the School of Industrial Arts "by the skin of my teeth." There, Mantilla studied art and met his first wife; the marriage was not entirely successful. "I got married when I was twenty-one, twenty-two. What the hell did I know about life?"

Mantilla's first professional job was with Eartha Kitt. He was twenty-one, but not ready. "I had just gotten married. I was very happy. The gig lasted about two or three weeks. I did the job fairly well, but not like a professional. I didn't have that much experience." Kitt got sick, took time off, and never rehired Mantilla. He continued to gather experience in a way traditional for a Latin musician, going into the Catskill Mountain resorts with a band. "I played timbales, but most of the time it was congas only—six nights a week—Grossinger's or the Concord or the different hotels. Everybody starts out there."

Now Mantilla sees these jobs as crucial because "you have to get respect among your peers before you can do anything. The Latin thing was part of me. I was brought up in it and if I didn't do that, there'd be no jumping off spot. I had to do the Latin thing because it has to do with the rhythms." Everything comes back to the traditional configurations that Mantilla grew up with and adapted, whether Puerto Rican, Cuban or jazz-related Latin rhythms: "I played with the best

Latin bands; I know my roots and I know my rhythms. Some people just play and they figure that's it. It's not. There's nothing like the actual experience of the culture." And not merely of one culture, because Cuban and Puerto Rican musics have distinct rhythms. "They have a different bounce to their music. The syncopation is different. I think the Cuban music has more of a strong 4/4 feel. Puerto Rican music is more bouncy. The Brazilian music hooks up in a different way too: it's all in two, but a different syncopation." Mantilla also plays in a "jazz way"—with less of a 4/4 feeling, giving a primary pulse to every eighth beat, a practice that allows more flexibility. Each mode is taxing, and despite twenty-six years of experience Mantilla makes few extravagant claims about certain aspects of his playing: "I've been playing pretty good at most of this stuff, even at my Puerto Rican thing. I'm not that great at it, but I can do it."

Mantilla was introduced to jazz by Ray Barretto. "When I met Ray he was playing jazz, and I was in the Latin thing. Barretto hadn't any idea how to play Latin conga till he met me and we started hanging out. He was a guy who learned how to play in the army style and he was playing with the jazz beboppers." Barretto's example was fortunate for several reasons. Mantilla felt he was recording too many sessions for which he got no recognition. Distressed by the backbiting competition among the Latin players, he also wanted more artistic freedom. "People still call me for salsa recordings, but those companies don't give you anything. They pay you under scale and they don't give you social security and unemployment. Mongo, Ray Barretto, Tito Puente—they stood that for years. The only way you can make a good living as a Latin percussionist is to get your own records, have your own group, and start producing."

The competition in the Latin musical community has not always been healthy. "When I came up, there were kids in their twenties and they'd say, 'What the hell, that guy can't play. I'll burn him up.' That's how it is in this business. So you've got to go and perform, top-notch, as much as you can and act as a gentleman. Sometimes, when you start getting too close to people, they start cutting you. I got out of that. I'm in my own situation and everybody that helps me, I love it."

Mantilla's developing style has created problems for him. Most Latin bands are relatively conservative musically, and his friends were suspicious about Mantilla's innovations. "The Latin thing gets bogged down after a while," Mantilla maintains. "They say, 'You're not playing that right,' or 'That's a jazz lick. . .You can't do it.' Being from New York City and with all that's going on around me, I'm not going to get tied up in my own little box. That's why I had to get out. That's why I like playing jazz. It's a free thing. It's like meeting new people all the time. It's international. So I started my direction elsewhere, making my own situations where people call me as a personality by myself."

The turning point came in 1960 when Mantilla was offered a job with flutist Herbie Mann, who was traveling at that point with two or three percussionists, including at various times Mantilla, Barretto, Patato Valdes, Chief Bey and the African drummer Michael Olatunji. Mantilla recorded a series of albums with Mann, including two live sets at the Village Gate. Mantilla left the group to form a Latin band with Barretto: "He can talk you into anything."

In 1963 Mantilla took his family to Puerto Rico for what turned out to be a seven-year stay. He was an addict. "I had a big bout with the drug scene at the time that Parker, everybody was into it. If you weren't snorting something, or weren't shooting up, you weren't hip. Well, after my band with Barretto, I was into it lightly. I was making money and doing well. I was about twenty-eight. I went to Puerto Rico to try to get away from it and it only got worse.

"I went down with style—I brought my own Latin band. It was lucky I played drums, because in Puerto Rico everybody played congas. I met a few promoters and ended up switching from regular timbales and hand drums to traps, playing shows in the different hotels. You had to wait in line to get a job playing congas, so I started playing drums. That saved my life over there. Then after a while I began to play congas, but I really strung out. Puerto Rico was hot and those people just slowed me down. I spent up a storm. I had a house. I was with my first wife and my baby was growing up. I think I was just too young to settle down. It takes a man to realize that you're going to bring your family down. I said, 'Listen, I got to leave because in the long run you're going to hate me.' So I left them. I left them to come back to New York to try to get straight. For a while I was a vagabond. For eight to nine years nobody knew who Ray Mantilla was. I had to start from scratch again. I went into the mountains. Grossinger's again." A woman he met in the mountains convinced Mantilla to get on methadone.

Mantilla's next break came by chance—he met drummer Art Blakey at a bar and together they reminisced about the shows Mantilla had done with Herbie Mann at New York's Apollo Theater. Not everything in the shows appealed to Mantilla, despite the Latin public's enthusiasm for Mann's music. He remembers the way Olatunji impressed the audience with his African robes and imposing mannerisms. As a result, "I had to get into a show bag. I would take off my jacket and get on top of the chair and put the bongos between my legs and play them with sticks and jump around and he would go, 'Oh yeah' and then he would take his robe and throw it on the floor. And we brought the house down. That was something. But then and there, I swore that, if I ever make it, I don't want to do no show. I just want to sit down and play my instrument." Blakey offered Mantilla a job on one condition—that he get off methadone. "I was saying, 'My God, maybe somebody up there likes me.' "

Mantilla had already recorded several selections of master drummer Max Roach's *Freedom Now! Suite*, recorded in 1960. After two years with Blakey, Roach again called Mantilla to take part in his percussion ensemble "M'Boom." Mantilla admires both Blakey and Roach: "Roach is such a technician. He's such a precise drummer. He's so aware and he's so powerful. He makes you get up and just look with respect. Just respect the way that he plays his drums and knows what he's doing. Art is more of a primitive player. He plays and he's bashing out. Art Blakey is more like me—the street. We just bash out." Mantilla was challenged by Roach's ensemble: "We had seven drummers together, not just playing bebop, but playing different time signatures. It all had to do with polyrhythms, like numbers. You take one number across one line and another across another line, and it has to get together somewhere along the line, for one bar, and then goes out again."

Mantilla has been back eight years now, rebuilding his reputation, recording and performing everything from disco to avant-garde sessions. "I went with Gato Barbieri for a while and I did some of his records, and some studio dates. They call you and you don't even know who is doing the dates sometimes. I like to be more personal with the leaders and understand the music and understand them. The studio gigs are not the same as if you know the guy for a while and go to each other's house and listen." Mantilla prefers to work with those he calls "his people": the friends and musicians he trusts and admires. One of these people is David Amram, the talented musician who took Mantilla to Cuba, a trip documented on Amram's *Flying Fish* record. Mantilla enjoys working folk festivals with Amram too: "Amram's taught me that all music is beautiful and is great. Even one guy playing the guitar, if he's got something good—you can tell. Dulcimers, soulful music, it makes me very receptive. I can relate very easily to a lot of people and it's like being in a band."

Mantilla sees his role in a band as helping people stay together. "I'm the hand drummer. I've got to relate to everything around me and put it together with a nice bow and package it up and present it. I'm like that— little ingredients, the salt and the pepper. Without it, something's missing and that's been my function— putting friends together, coordinating things."

JAZZ LIVES

Mantilla's first record as a leader illustrates this process: each of his musicians—Carl Ratzer, Joe Chambers, Jeremy Steig, and Eddie Gomez—has been a leader in his own right: Mantilla has played on their records. He calls these men "part of my family." "When you've got a gig, you call your people." *Mantilla*, the drummer's Inner City recording, features compositions by drummer Joe Chambers, guitarist Ratzer and a piece in 7/4 by Jeremy Steig. If anything, Mantilla's part in the recording is too decorous—he plays in a short percussion exchange with Chambers at the beginning, and solos at greater length on "Seven for Mantilla." The recording is pleasant, but it could use a little more of the bashing "street" style Mantilla talks about.

Despite a gall bladder attack that temporarily stopped him, Mantilla feels he's back on the right track, coordinating people and making things happen. It's been a "rough trip," but "at forty-four I'm glad I have an expectation. I don't want to be a superstar. I just want to make a decent living. I want to have my own little group of people that listen to my music. Gato's got his people that listen to Gato and Barretto's got his people and Puente's got his people. So I'll have Mantilla's people. Because my friends are all going to become big stars, and they're all going to go their way again. I've got to end up being on my own."

ANTHONY BRAXTON

In 1965, when the jazz world was dominated by hard bop on the one hand and "free jazz" on the other, a group of musicians formed in Chicago under the rubric of AACM, the Association for the Advancement of Creative Musicians. Intensity and energy were the critical attributes of the free players, and "soul" the standard by which one judged the hard boppers; the Chicago musicians offered something different: they were equally interested in free and composed music. Some talked about escaping the "trap" of a constant rhythm, while others sought a discipline unpopular with the free players. All played a large variety of instruments. One of the important groups to emerge from the Chicago organization was the Creative Construction Company, which featured the violin of Leroy Jenkins, Leo Smith's brass, pianist Richard Abrams, and on saxophones native Chicagoan Anthony Braxton. Now the most celebrated performer and composer in the new jazz to come out of Chicago, Anthony Braxton confronts the world with a startled, wide-eyed Orphan Annie look. Like the other AACM musicians, Braxton uses space and silence in his music, and occasionally does without a rhythm section altogether. He is as concerned with bringing wit and intelligence into his music as he is with expending energy playing it, and is so serious about composing that he calls himself only "40 percent an instrumentalist."

Born in 1945, Braxton has in the last decade recorded close to thirty albums as a leader, including a three-record, fully notated piece for multiple orchestras issued by Arista. That piece calls for 160 musicians and four conductors; but Braxton has also created several solo saxophone albums, recorded duets with guitarist Derek Bailey, pianist Muhal Richard Abrams, saxophonists Joseph Jarman and Roscoe Mitchell, and percussionist Max Roach, written for a big band, and played such instruments as the contrabass clarinet, sopranino saxophone, accordion, harmonica, musette, and assorted bells, chimes and percussion instruments. The second floor of his home in Woodstock, New York contains several shiny metal garbage cans—he has put motors in some in an attempt to force them to make music. In his study Braxton works on four projects arranged on large easels encircling his chair. When I was there, he was composing solo piano music, a work for his quartet, and pieces for six and ten orchestras. The overwhelming variety of Braxton's activities suggests randomness—but the impression is false. Since he was nine or ten, living in a tough neighborhood in south Chicago and shocked to find that he was different from his friends and family, Braxton has marched purposefully to the beat of a different drummer, intent both on creating his own musical universe and on connecting it with the outside world. In the notes to his multiorchestral album, Braxton tells how he was inspired by the big band battles of the past, but also by the movement of bands in parades, by Charles Ives's *Fourth Symphony*, and by works of Stockhausen, Xenakis and Cage. Braxton was one of the first black avant-garde musicians to acknowledge a debt to contemporary European music. He feels a need to be original, but also to fight the sense of isolation such originality has imposed upon him. His work is not unique: there is something corresponding to multiorchestralism, he writes, in "every

Anthony Braxton *by Michael Ullman*

culture. This medium can be experienced all over the planet."

Braxton is interested in science and technology, but also in astrology, a discipline dedicated to drawing connections, however tenuous, between our actions and a larger world. He once supported himself by hustling chess: the world of chess, he says, is magical and seductive. "Playing chess is just like creating music. There is this whole universe, and there are laws to this universe. There's justice and certain moves will make certain responses. Certain situations have to be dealt with creatively. You move and you complete your objective and checkmate a person. It's a just universe. It's wonderful, so exciting. My heart beats, the possibilities are so exciting." Braxton has discovered that the more creative he becomes, the more closely he will be in touch both with a "wonderful universe" and with other people.

His music, once scorned and ignored by jazz critics because it doesn't "swing" or is too "cold," is now reaching larger audiences, thanks largely to his contract with Arista Records. Braxton's saxophone style, with its ragged lines, wide skips and abrupt silences, is now rightly seen in the context of Charlie Parker and Eric Dolphy. Although his playing can be intense, he considers that intensity a device to be used appropriately rather than the ultimate end of music. As a young man he imitated Paul Desmond, worshipped John Coltrane and was transformed by Schoenberg. Today his compositions owe as much to the "classical" avant-garde as to the black traditions in music. Inevitably, they reflect his own systematic thinking: Braxton characteristically develops series of works, each reflecting a different aspect of a compositional principle such as the repetition of a rhythmic line. Ideally Braxton's multiorchestral piece should be performed for an audience grouped between bands. His goal, he says, is to create a way for people to experience his music as a "living and breathing universe." He has projected several series of such compositions, each more grandiose than the last—the fifth work in Series A involves one hundred orchestras connected by satellite television systems, while the fourth in the next series, to be completed in the year 2000, should include several galaxies.

Braxton lives with his wife and child and several collies in a rural part of Woodstock, a contrast to the urban neighborhood in which he was born. "I grew up on 67th and Michigan. I came from a poor family—not really impoverished—we had enough food to eat. But my reality was the reality of the south side and I couldn't understand what was happening there. Seeing my friends getting killed in gangs—the whole intensity of life in the south side at that time, it was hard for me to have an affinity with. For instance, many of my friends learned the concept of hip. I never could quite be the right kind of hip. I never seemed to follow the same track that everybody was following, even if I wanted to. I'd be trying to be like everybody else, but it never quite worked out. So I grew up feeling somewhat unhappy about being on the planet and not quite understanding what I was dealing with. I don't want to paint a picture of the child who is miserable, but I recall growing up with an intense desire to figure out what I was really dealing with. I was and I still am very affected by the physical reality of black people and what minority people are dealing with in this country. As a child I'd turn on the television and see one reality, but then I'd go outside and I'd see another."

Braxton took what he thought were positive steps to handle his problem. He read books; he played chess; he listened to music. Literacy didn't help him become hip, but his family, particularly his older brother, was pleased when he took up the alto saxophone: "When I first started listening to music, I had Paul Desmond records. My family was very happy. My brother said music was very nice, as long as it didn't get out of hand. Especially since it was pretty. After a year of listening to Paul Desmond, I went over to my friend Tommy's house, and his father said, 'You're listening to Desmond. That's nice, but first listen to this record.' It was called *The Shape of Things to Come*—Ornette

Coleman. He said, 'This is where the music's going.' I took it home and played it and said, 'Oh my God, this is horrible.' I gave it back and the next couple days, I woke up thinking about the record. Couldn't sleep. Went back, borrowed the record again, played it and, 'Um, I don't understand this music. It sounds very strange, but there's something about it I like.' For me that meant looking at the liner notes and finding out who the author was talking about. Who's related to Ornette Coleman? Cecil Taylor." When Braxton brought home a Cecil Taylor record, he no longer made his family happy: "I was twelve or thirteen. Immediate separation between me and my family, me and my brothers. Everybody thought I was kidding. I didn't know what the problem was. This was the music I liked. That was the beginning of our separation. Same with chess. Same with mathematics."

Listeners attuned to Braxton's erratic saxophone runs will be surprised at his interest in Paul Desmond's style, with its emphasis on tone and smooth legato lines. Nevertheless, Braxton calls Desmond and John Coltrane the two "strongest musical draws I've encountered." As an adolescent, he imitated Desmond: "I used to play like Desmond—lean on pianos and play 'Take Five.' I've always been somewhat of an extremist anyway, and when I would dig somebody I would go all the way. Even though I didn't need glasses, I bought glasses and became witty." Desmond's playing, not his celebrated wit, convinced Braxton to take up the saxophone. "There was something about Desmond's music that opened doors for me, because I do recall hearing a record of Charlie Parker's before and I just didn't like it. It didn't make any sense to me. I heard a John Coltrane record before I heard Paul Desmond and it didn't make any sense to me. I thought they were interesting, but they frightened me a bit. Then I heard Paul Desmond. It clicked.

"Just before then I was going to play the trumpet in high school because I wanted to be like Miles Davis, but Desmond's music was the deciding factor. He was an extremely disciplined improviser. It is difficult to play at the pace Desmond normally functions—very slow—and really invent and not waste a note. He had to be an extremely disciplined man in his approach to the music. I learned something from Desmond—I try to approach my activity in a very disciplined way, even as an improviser, not to play anything that is not real. My progression in music has never been to start at the earliest point and then go to the most contemporary. In fact, I usually start near the middle and work forward and backward at the same time." (Braxton's record shelf now features a huge box of Stockhausen beside an equally impressive collection of Fats Waller.) "So I discovered Charlie Parker much later than I discovered Paul Desmond. Before Desmond I listened to Frankie Lyman and Bill Haley and Little Richard. That was the music I was initially intrigued with, and then I went from that to Ahmad Jamal."

From 1959 to 1964 Braxton had an admirable teacher in Jack Gell, then of the Chicago School of Music. Gell is a disciplined man, now in Los Angeles, who taught Braxton the basics of music and the technique of the saxophone. As an instrumentalist Braxton was also influenced, he says, by Lee Konitz, Jackie McLean and Eric Dolphy. Ornette Coleman's ideas affected him more than Coleman's alto sax technique. "What I admired about musicians like Desmond and Coltrane and Dolphy was the fact that they didn't play like anybody else. They believed in what they did." Hearing Eric Dolphy for the first time was a shock. Braxton was immediately impressed by Dolphy's speed; he had been expecting something more like Ornette Coleman. "I used to frequent a record shop on 58th Street in Chicago, four or five blocks from my house. I saw this record *Outward Bound* by Eric Dolphy. By this time I'd become very, very interested in the music of Ornette Coleman. But the record came on and when the solo started, 'It didn't say it had a violin on the record.' It was Eric Dolphy playing so fast, it sounded like a violin. I liked him immediately and later found out Eric was a Gemini. His tendencies were attractive to me. But I never met him and I never saw him play live."

Around 1963 Braxton met John Coltrane, whom he revered. "Coltrane was quiet and gentle until he got on the stage. His music was so robust, so dynamic, it was frightening. I was never friends with Coltrane from the standpoint of 'Let's be on the same level.' I was like a student and I would not let him treat me in any other way. He invited me to sit in with him and I wouldn't do it because I saw too many people sitting in with Coltrane. I felt I was much stronger than them as a musician but Coltrane was like a god in my eyes and it wouldn't have been respectful for me to play with the man when I wasn't on his level. I used to call him Mr. Coltrane." Braxton has said that Coltrane was as intense as any player could be, and that it is useless to imitate that intensity, as hundreds of saxophonists have done. Despite the lure of Trane's personality and the power of his music, Braxton backed away from this influence: "I didn't want to play like Desmond or Coltrane or Dolphy, because the thing I admired about them most was the fact that they created their own universe. If you could grab Coltrane's music and graph it, you'd see a certain shape. Same with Dolphy. Desmond's music was kind of like that but still melodic. [Braxton makes a soft, wavy motion with his arm; Dolphy's music elicits a faster, jerkier motion. When demonstrating his own music, Braxton's arm suddenly acts as though it has been captured by a silent movie: it moves too fast to be comfortable and jumps around surprisingly.] Well, for my music I designed a language. It was the first kind of improvisational language that would move with such sharp curves. My rhythmic structure was deliberately reshaped. My playing is much more pointed even than Dolphy's, because I utilize another relationship to primary pulse in music. That aspect of my music made it difficult for the jazz critics to relate to my music. That's the distinguishing feature that they write about."

At the height of his interest in Coltrane, Braxton heard a piece by Arnold Schoenberg. Schoenberg's advanced harmonic sense, his discipline, use of space and relative rhythmic freedom affected Braxton immediately. It was Schoenberg's early Op. 11, *Three Pieces for Piano* (1909) "that floored me. I couldn't believe it. I had been studying music for ten years; my involvement with Russian art music was interesting, but it was an activity that didn't have anything to do with my life. It wasn't concerned with black people. I would play Bach, Vivaldi and Beethoven. I enjoyed it but it didn't touch me inside that much. Schoenberg's music completely knocked me out, changed my whole life. It made me reconsider everything I'd ever considered before. I went back and started dealing with Beethoven and Bach and I'm still dealing with Beethoven and Bach and also it opened up Anton Webern and later Stockhausen and Cage."

Soon after, Braxton entered Wilson Junior College, where he met Roscoe Mitchell and Jack DeJohnette, and then the Army, where in 1964 and 1965 Braxton played in bands and started to lead small groups. "I started having problems in the Army. I would play the music they wanted me to play: we'd play classical music, and marches. It was clear that I was a proficient technician. What wasn't clear to them, however, was the music I really wanted to play. For instance, my parents sent me Albert Ayler's record *Bells* and Coltrane's *Ascension*. I played the records and after five minutes everybody in the barracks came and was ready to kill me. Because I was attracted to this kind of music people thought they couldn't like me. Fortunately, I was able to have some friends who could relate to some of the activity I was into."

One of these people was a forty-year-old sergeant named Joe Stevenson. "He played practically every instrument except for brass. So I began taking lessons from him on alto saxophone. He wanted to clarify certain technical things. He'd sit and talk to me about the music and he became so interested in my composing that he joined my quartet. He was a very rare person. Not many people would lend themselves like that to another person. Especially since I was studying with him. I practiced more than anybody in the organization. I used to get up at six o'clock to practice before first formation. After the day was over I'd go over and rehearse. He was aware of how hard I'd practiced, and he thought, 'Why shouldn't he be able to play what he wants to play, as long as he is taking care of the business of the Army band too?' "

After his Army stint, Braxton returned to Chicago because he knew the sympathetic Roscoe Mitchell would be there. Braxton found Mitchell immediately, and "the very next day, he took me down to the AACM where I joined up to become a member. For the first time in my life, I would meet a group of people who were interested in some of the things I was interested in. Even if they weren't interested in all of it, at least they wouldn't call me crazy. I was tired of feeling like I was crazy. It was a pivotal point in my life. There were a lot of new ideas and communication. People were trying everything they could think of. There were two or three concerts every week. Everyone would do something different, and the feeling was very conducive to new discoveries." The Chicagoans seemed less driven than contemporary New York players: interested in changing the image of the contemporary black musician, they did not want to be seen merely as virtuosos on one instrument—they attacked all instruments and made new ones. They played "sounds" rather than choruses: Roscoe Mitchell's first album was entitled *Sound*, and J. B. Figi described it as "an exploration of the possibilities of unorthodox, yet meaningful, sounds inherent in the instruments." The Art Ensemble of Chicago traveled with a truckload of instruments. Whitney Balliett wryly described a concert to which they arrived late, suggesting that the unpacking of those instruments was their first piece. The Chicago groups were interested in other arts as well; Braxton has written a quartet piece for Merce Cunningham, and the Art Ensemble, with their costumes, African paint and props, add theatrical spice to their performances.

Braxton's first recording, *Three Compositions of New Jazz*, was made with Leroy Jenkins, Leo Smith and Muhal Richard Abrams—the Creative Construction Company. Two of the compositions are Braxton's. His titles are eccentric: usually they consist of letters and numbers connected by lines. Sometimes he includes geometrical figures; in any case they convey little to anyone besides Braxton himself. The titles reflect Braxton's fascination with numbers, with mathematics, and also something of his distrust of impressionism and cheap political-spiritual uses of music. His work, he says, has spiritual implications. All music does, but he was offended by the imitations of Coltrane prevalent in the late '60s: "We already had *A Love Supreme*; why do we need somebody chanting 'supreme love' or something like that? There's a lot of pseudo-spiritualism that came up post-Coltrane. Mysticism and spiritualism became big business. I heard some people talk about spiritualism and turned around and found them involved in some of the most negative things you could ever imagine. Throughout that period I just separated myself. My activity was completely isolated from everybody's in that regard."

With drummer Billy Hart, Braxton visited New York City, but the saxophonists there all sounded like Coltrane, and he felt that few would be interested in his music. No one, it seemed, knew about Stockhausen or John Cage. Braxton played with Sam Rivers's big band—"a wonderful experience for me"—but in 1969 he left for Paris with the Creative Construction Company. In Europe "nobody liked the Creative Construction Company. They appreciated us as individuals and our seeming ability, but nobody could relate to us. We didn't have a bass and the music just didn't go like anybody else's. They received the Art Ensemble of Chicago with open arms. The Art Ensemble had a very dynamic music but somehow people were attracted to it. Our music was perceived as being cold, and that has stuck with me."

Soon after Braxton returned to the United States, he found himself living with Ornette Coleman. "He happened to hear us when I was in Paris and he liked the group. He invited me to come when I was in New York. I stayed with him while I was trying to get myself together in New York. Soon I got a little apartment, a practice place on West Third St., and I stayed there working on woodwind quintets until I got so interested in the chess scene. Then I would wake up at four o'clock in the morning, read *The New York Times*, practice chess games, study 500 pounds of books, Robert Burns, and then go out to hustle my game of chess in Washington Square Park." At the time it seemed easier to make a living through chess than through music. For a year, Braxton gave up music.

Then one night Leroy Jenkins called Braxton and asked him to take part in a final concert by the Creative Construction Company. "We gave a concert at the Washington Square Peace Church, and Jack De-Johnette came. He liked the music so much that right after the concert he insisted that we go someplace and sit in and do some playing. So we went to the Village Vanguard. Chick Corea, Dave Holland and Barry Altschul were playing and we sat in with them. Right after that, Chick asked me to come by his house and jam with him. So I started going over to Chick's house with all my scores. I had all of Stockhausen, Boulez, Xenakis's piano music and Schoenberg. Being the incredible musician that he is, Chick played the music."

As a result of these informal contacts, Corea asked Braxton to join the group called Circle. It lasted from 1970 to 1972. Unquestionably Corea's most adventurous undertaking, at the beginning of its career Circle featured primarily spontaneous improvisations. The group achieved some limited commercial success, but Corea broke it up, and there were bad feelings between Braxton and Corea as a result: "When I first met him, he was fixing to quit Miles [Davis] because Miles was doing more commercial music. Chick was interested in more contemporary kinds of music, with more open forms. Another use of language. But then he changed. Scientology had a great deal to do with it. But I don't want to put it all on Scientology. [Braxton is more apt to blame Corea's sudden change of heart on the fact that he is a Gemini.]

When he changed his mind, the direction he wanted to go in encroached on what I wanted to do. I did not want to stand up there and play bossa nova. I did not want to play a commercial kind of creative music. I don't think he realized the nature of the struggle sometimes. It can be very intense trying to find enough money to live on. When you're playing the kind of music that I'm playing, certain avenues aren't open to you. I wanted to quit the group in New York before we went back out to California. Chick convinced me to stay in the group, but when we got out to California he changed his mind and broke the group up, stranding me in California. Outside of that, Circle was a nice experience."

Back in New York City in 1972, Braxton made his concert debut at Town Hall, performing with a duet, trio and quintet. Then, after another stay in Paris, he returned to New York, moving to Woodstock in 1975. His Arista recordings have provided him a larger audience without affording him an active performing career. Braxton is philosophical about this restriction: "I imagine to grow up in various places in the country, like Iowa or something, where you are at the mercy of the media or forces which control the kind of information we get, is to be in a very peculiar position. Because at least in New York, a person might venture outside his or her environment and hear some activity which has not been sanctioned by the media. But in many parts of the country the musicians never get a chance to play."

Still, Braxton plays regularly in the major cities in the east, usually with a quartet and sometimes as a solo saxophonist. His solo concerts are fascinating if demanding. Braxton is always an orderly player, though anyone who has seen him hunched over his alto saxophone in concert, his legs bent at the knees and his left arm flapping with the beat, will hesitate to call him a "cold" performer. He is aware of the need for both variety and overt structure if an audience is to follow a solo saxophone. In a recent concert he played versions of "Basin St. Blues" and other standards alongside his own compositions. At times his playing had a slapdash vigor; elsewhere it had an odd slithering quality as he slipped up and down a scale. Braxton can be angular, straightforward or sly. His pieces are often founded on some kind of repetition: a Dolphyesque line will form a theme; it will be repeated, inverted, varied in every possible way, but the piece will constantly reflect the shape of its cell or theme. Another piece may investigate a particular saxophone technique: Braxton may restrict himself to overblowing or playing in the altissimo range of his alto. Braxton can be lyrical, but he eschews the fluency of a Phil Woods. (Playing the bop classic "Donna Lee" at a bone-rattling tempo, Braxton sounds as if he were tripping down stairs, catching himself at the last moment.)

Braxton has been lucky in his accompanists. His regular quartet includes David Holland on bass and Barry Altschul on percussion, as well as such horn players as trumpeter Kenny Wheeler and trombonist George Lewis. Holland, a virtuoso who has played with Miles Davis and Circle and still performs with Sam Rivers, is limber and energetic but, like Braxton, orderly. Altschul is a crisp, precise drummer, extraordinarily quick and inventive: one Braxton recording opens with a boppish unison chorus, followed by an eerie metallic sound—the first chorus of Altschul's drum solo begins with his drawing the bow against the edge of the cymbal. Wheeler is a relatively conservative player, while Chicagoan George Lewis is the most important trombonist since Grachan Moncur and Roswell Rudd. Lewis, as witty and eccentric as Braxton himself, can also play a gut-bucket blues. He shares many of Braxton's interests. I heard them at a club during their first engagement together; in the middle of a piece, Lewis played a phrase that hinted at a Sousa march. Surprised, Braxton looked up and then countered with an equally oblique suggestion. They trembled on the edge of parody until taking the plunge, dragging drummer Altschul into an effective, though raucous, distillation of a ragged Sousa march. By the end, even the austere Altschul was smiling.

Braxton can be playful, but he likes to be systematic.

He has developed, for instance, series of compositions based on three principles of repetition, which he calls Kelvin, Colbolt and Kaufman. In the Kelvin series, the improviser is given a rhythmic shape or pattern. That shape (or cell or germ) is the source of the piece, but the improviser uses it in different ways, depending on the number of the composition: Braxton has composed Kelvin 3 up to 500. He describes Colbolt as "a group dealing with sound block patterns. We used to do Colbolt compositions within the group Circle. That particular area of my work was put together around 1969. I got it by studying fireflies—and the sound in the light goes like that." In the Colbolt series an orchestra might play a chord repeatedly; each time it is played something within the chord is changed—what will change depends on the series. The interest of such a piece is in the changing textures of sound. While Braxton says Colbolt has never been recorded, parts of his multiorchestral piece do illustrate the technique. The last series, Kaufman, is like Kelvin except that each cell involves more than one line, more than one event. Whereas Kelvin keeps the same shape, Kaufman has more than one cell and includes some "repetition" cells. "The distinguishing factor of Kaufman has to do with its use of space, its use of counterpoint, whereas Kelvin is the use of a particular germ."

As Braxton notes, it is this interest in methodology that "turns jazz critics off and makes it difficult sometimes for me to have my activity viewed in its real context." But much of his music is more accessible than such critics might suggest. The jazz fan who listens to *New York Fall 1974* will hear a boppish unison melody played over a steady rhythm, while the two sides of *Duets 1976* open with "Maple Leaf Rag" and the Dolphy classic "Miss Ann." Braxton's orchestral work is heard on Arista 4080, which includes a stunning recreation of a march—the performance stalls deliberately in the middle during a "free" section, but ends with Jon Faddis squeaking on a piccolo trumpet over a high-stepping ensemble. The performance has been called a parody, but there is no sniggering here: Braxton likes march music. The multiorchestral piece contains no improvisation. Braxton is interested in the way sound moves—he moves a phrase from one orchestra to another, or from one side of my living room to another, depending on how I look at it. A live performance would make this aspect of the work more impressive, but as recorded the piece is often fascinating and always intelligent.

Braxton today has a following that at times seems fanatical. A reviewer for *Coda* magazine called his article on Braxton the most important thing he had done in his life, and I have no doubt that there are countless teenagers who are cultivating a wide-eyed look, affecting cardigan sweaters, and learning to stutter on an alto sax in order to be like Anthony Braxton. Reading his liner notes, one might think that Braxton's music is easier to comprehend than his spoken language. In his comments on the multiorchestral piece, he writes about "projections," which his editor clarifies by putting "Forms" in parentheses beside it. He is self-educated, stubborn and sometimes obscure, but on some level he always makes sense, and his single-minded devotion to his art is inspiring. He's hip now, because we've come to him. As he said to me at the end of our long talk, "I've been talking a lot about the significance of various systems and activities. Of course I'll continue to talk about that, if you'd like. But it's no less real for me than Phil Woods's lyricism. My particular path in creativity was taken as honestly as I could take a path. It's really just how I am. I make no apologies. I work hard and I intend to continue to work hard for my viewpoint, and to learn and discover. That's who I am. That's what I am."

STEVE BACKER

When he learned that Clive Davis, once the head of CBS Records, was founding Arista Records, Steve Backer went to Davis with some suggestions. Backer, then the general manager of ABC/Impulse, was ready for a new challenge: "I said to him that I wanted to put together a wide-spectrum, multidimensional approach to jazz for him and that if he wanted to get involved with me, I wouldn't be limited to any one genre: either sheerly commercial or sheerly aesthetic, avant-garde or mainstream, or crossover or acoustic. I told him it was going to be a balanced approach to the music. That is the only healthy approach to take from a commercial point of view because one never knows where the music is going to go." The scope of his plans and their practicality are typical of Backer. A trim, modish, youthful-looking man just into his forties, he has the business and political skills to thrive in a large corporation—it's like "a game of chess," he told me. He also has the wide-ranging tastes that make his approach possible. Although the first thing he did at Arista was to sign Anthony Braxton—after five years, Braxton's records are still only marginally profitable for the company—Backer has also put together a line of more "accessible" jazz musicians, such as the Brecker brothers, Larry Coryell and Norman Connors, as well as a series by frankly funk-oriented artists. Under

Backer's direction, Arista bought up and has started to reissue the famous Savoy series, which includes some of the greatest recordings of Charlie Parker, and the English Freedom label, dedicated largely to avant-garde artists. Arista created the GRP label, which produces mostly "crossover," and recently the Novus label.

Backer is proud of his accomplishments with Arista—proud of having produced a three-record Anthony Braxton orchestral piece and proud of being able to adapt to the conditions of the business he works in. A more conventional businessman than John Snyder, he is able to maintain his position because he "hasn't led the company down the drain. I've become sophisticated about knowing how not to have the rug pulled out from under me on a business level. I understand what my investment has to be with each artist, with each genre that I'm working within, and what my return on each investment is going to be, so I don't record artists philanthropically." Backer is interested in exploiting, not reforming, the recording industry. A corporation, he says, is only "a large bunch of people," open to many forms of persuasion. He's persuaded Arista to create a catalog of significant music—avante-garde and commercial—and demonstrated that one can work profitably within "the system." Not everyone would want to do so, but for Steve Backer a large company represents interesting challenges and important possibilities.

Steve Backer once wanted to become a jazz musician, but he realized he didn't have "the chops" and graduated from Hofstra with a business degree. In 1968 he was living in Paris running a travel business. During the national strike that paralyzed France, Backer's investors pulled out and he was unemployed.

"I decided I would try to get close to something I loved: music. I started working as a promotion executive for MGM and Verve Records, and then two years later I went with Electra Records. It was a fantastic background because you get to know the business inside and out: marketing, merchandising,

Steve Backer *by Barbara King*

promotion, advertising, distribution, retailing, artist development, artist relations, publicity—the gamut." Working on promotion, Backer learned a crucial lesson: a record company is a group of individuals, not the sinister mass some musicians consider it.

Backer was interested in inaugurating a budget jazz line at Electra Records to rival the successful classical series, Nonesuch, when he received an offer to join ABC/Impulse as the National Promotion Director in 1971. He took it. By the early '70s the Impulse line had become moribund; its most popular artist, John Coltrane, died in 1967 and interest waned in Trane's strident successors. Backer was hired to revive the company. He began by taking groups of Impulse artists on well-publicized tours; exposing large audiences to Keith Jarrett, Sam Rivers, Alice Coltrane, Pharoah Sanders and Michael White. The tours— almost unknown for jazz artists at the time—were "a great success promotionally and also in terms of stimulating awareness of the label and the artists. A tour like that loses a lot of money. It is financed by the corporation and tickets are sold at very low prices. The promotion is a long-term capital investment, but most companies have difficulty dealing with long-term concepts, basically because the music industry is so volatile. People are in and out, but to me the tours are part of a building process." The volatility of the music business has put a premium on instant success. Because the system works against relatively "inaccessible" jazz, it is difficult for an artist to plan a career. As a result, "continuity" has become one of Backer's key words.

Backer was general manager of Impulse from 1971 to 1974. During those years, Backer says, Impulse did what it could to support its musicians. Artist manager Maxine Gregg has said that companies, not musicians, sell records; Backer emphasizes "what people want to hear at a given time—that can be more important than what a company does for an artist. There are just too many variables that are beyond the company's control. I would say that probably 85 percent is what's in the grooves and the other 15 percent is what the company can do. Once you announce the records with advertising, once you get the record in the stores, once you try to get as much airplay as possible—not easy considering the sad state of radio in America—you've done what you can do. You can't force the consumer to walk into a store and buy the records."

A record company does not have control over the public's often fickle tastes. Today an album by Anthony Braxton or Cecil Taylor will sell at best 20,000 copies. John Coltrane's A Love Supreme sold ten times that number, Backer estimates, and Pharoah Sanders's Karma almost as many. The late '60s, a difficult time for mainstream jazz, he notes, made several avant-garde musicians wealthy, though the boom had little to do with the record companies' promotional departments. "In the '60s there were a lot of political things happening—the campus chaos, the Vietnam War—that pushed people to take a more serious approach to their music. To be able to get what Anthony Braxton or Cecil Taylor or Ornette Coleman are saying, you have to approach the music with as much seriousness as that artist brings to it. Now, people are dancing their troubles away to disco. People prefer crossover jazz because of its simplified rhythmic approach, its less sophisticated soloing, and the shorter solos. People today prefer not to work at their entertainment."

Nevertheless, Backer has continued to issue two Anthony Braxton recordings a year since signing him for Arista in 1974. "Braxton was living in France and wanted to come back to the States. I thought he was brilliant, so when he returned we negotiated a deal and began a long-term relationship. We've been able to maintain continuity with Braxton, a very adventurous, probing, but from a commercial point of view, a rather esoteric artist." Backer admires Braxton's music; as a businessman he also admires Braxton's "overview." "Braxton understands. He doesn't expect enormous consumer response. He's more concerned with the documentation of his music and with its reaching the widest number of people it can possibly reach under the circumstances."

In 1974 Braxton had recorded for several European labels as well as for the small Chicago company, Delmark. Interesting though it was, the music did not swing: Braxton was working outside regular meters and often without a drummer. As a producer, Backer is hesitant to suggest that an artist alter his approach, but when one seems receptive, Backer might explain a way to make the recording more acceptable. "There are things that not every artist is aware of. For instance, when you record for a major label and play one twenty-minute piece on each side, there is nothing that will be played on the radio. Even the sequencing of the record can turn off a lot of radio people. If you start with the more difficult material, the guy who listens to the albums at a station will never listen to the whole album to find the more accessible cut." For these reasons, Backer asked Ran Blake to record in a variety of settings rather than as a soloist, and he suggested that Braxton's first albums with Arista "deal with time and meter. Then we were able to make more people in the jazz community embrace his music. And then we went to the big band album that dealt with time also. That album won an award as the best of the year. From there Braxton went into various stretched-out, open-ended free improvisational approaches." The Braxton three-record set orchestral piece is an important milestone for Braxton, Backer and Arista, illustrating Backer's contention that major record companies have in fact been recording adventurous music. The scope of the Braxton project, scored for 160 musicians, makes it unique. "My pride in the project comes from the fact that I can't think of another instance where a black man, coming from the jazz tradition, has been allowed that kind of liberty, where that kind of money and that kind of energy have gone into a project with such limited commercial appeal."

Such recordings are made possible by those with commercial appeal, which generally means jazz-rock fusion. Backer does not merely record this music; he appreciates it. "It's not designed to be high art," he says. "It's calculated to be timely. I understand that the big problem is that a lot of jazz virtuosos have moved into the jazz-rock area and their playing is more limited in terms of virtuosity. That's their choice. I get upset when I keep reading things like, 'Why doesn't he play what he's capable of playing?' He's playing what he wants to play. Great musicians sometimes make bad fusion records. They might not understand the craft of fusion music, which is more about production craft. Sonny Rollins or Michael White or Benny Golson might not know how to make fusion records, but a lot of people do. And there are also a lot of bad bebop records and bad avant-garde records." Of course, no one produces a bad avant-garde record to make a lot of money, whereas some jazz musicians do make fusion records out of financial desperation. Critics are justifiably chagrined when talented musicians make records that move along as uncomfortably as an adult on a tricycle.

After distributing much of the English Freedom label, Arista started the Novus label. Arista would now wholly own the label under which they were to record their most challenging music. This system is more efficient economically, but there is a more subtle reason for the change: "A distributed label is recorded and built up in some other part of the world. But when the company's own personnel and money are directly involved in a recording project, there's more of a psychological investment on the part of the company personnel, from the top to the field people. It's just ego. They're closer to the music and they sell it better. There's not that back-of-the-bus attitude." A company is, after all, a group of people.

On that subject Backer differs with a number of the artists and managers who complain about the way the industry is set up. The business, Backer admits, "is structured very much in favor of the company rather than the artist. For instance, the company is given the option to extend an artist's contract. The artist has the option not to record if he doesn't want to. He does not have the option to record for someone else. You have to work within the confines of how it is and not how it ideally should be. With some artists, I have gotten into these rhetorical idealist discussions that can drive a person crazy. Because theoretically I agree with them. Due to the immense amount of rejection some artists have received in this country, they tend to become either hardened, embittered, on the one hand, or they transcend it in some spiritual way—as does Alice Coltrane with her whole religious approach." Not surprisingly, Backer is more attracted to the few musicians who, like Anthony Braxton, "come out of that rejection in a wholly logical, rational, pragmatic manner."

When I last talked to Backer, he had been walking around downtown Boston looking at the Arista records in the retail stores—doing field work of a sort. An executive of a large New York-based company, he lives in New Hampshire "in the interest of balance and in the interest of creative autonomy. The most profound thing the Rolling Stones ever said was, 'You get what you need.' You don't always get what you want, but you get what you need. I needed to do that."

Backer seeks to balance creativity and continuity in the music he is associated with. Rather than revive an old master, Backer would unearth a young star. "To me it's much more vital, much more important to deal with tomorrow in terms of jazz than yesterday." And so, Backer works to develop audiences for the relatively few musicians he can support. Despite periodic revaluations of his work, Backer is confident about the future of his part of Arista Records. "We're just as prolific at this point and as productive as we were five years ago. So the most important thing is the continuity. That's what I'm trying to stretch and emphasize. I can't think of anything else as vital."

CHARLES MINGUS

Charles Mingus succumbed to amyotropic lateral sclerosis, "Lou Gehrig's disease," on January 5, 1979, after a protracted, courageous struggle with the crippling ailment that finally caused his heart to fail. Of Mingus's last months, pianist-arranger Sy Johnson told Michael Cuscuna: "I've never known anybody like him when he was healthy, and I've certainly never known anyone like him when he was sick." Confined to a wheelchair during his last year, Mingus continued to compose and conduct, humming a series of melodies into a tape recorder for a session by folk singer Joni Mitchell, and sitting in an Atlantic recording studio where he exhorted and encouraged musicians who were realizing Mingus compositions he himself would never get to play.

Mingus was a larger-than-life figure who forced his musicians and audiences to live up to his passionate expectations. He was known to fire a band member on stage, lecture an unruly audience, glare at an erring section man or holler at a soloist who was faking it. He defied classification to the end. He was a bebop bassist who titled one of his records *Pre-Bird*. He was a sophisticated musician who played downhome blues as they have never been played before: with Mingus the blues could shriek, bubble, swing, or explode; he said he couldn't play "Haitian Fight Song" without thinking of racial injustice and hatred. He wrote the delicately mournful tribute to the departed Lester Young, "Goodbye Porkpie Hat," as well as the satirical "Fables of Faubus," dedicated to the reactionary governor. In his autobiography, Mingus wrote, "I'm going to play the truth of what I am." Rarely has the truth been so inspiring. As Mingus's widow said: "He made you live at the top of yourself."

Mingus was always interested in communicating, and when he wasn't playing or composing he was talking or writing. Several times in his career he appealed directly to his fans. One of his records, *Mingus at Monterey*, included a letter from Mingus asking that his listeners send money to offset his disastrous financial condition. *Let My Children Hear Music* offers an essay by Mingus defining the role of the composer in jazz, extolling the musical abilities of unrecognized black musicians, and praying to the public to let his children hear music: "For God's sake, rid this society of some of the noise so that those who have ears will be able to use them some place listening to good music." For some twenty years, Mingus was writing an autobiography, finally printed as *Beneath the Underdog: His World as Composed by Mingus*, an astonishing, elliptical memoir, full of scurrilous and finally boring anecdotes about Mingus's sex life, touching stories about his (of course) unhappy childhood, and comical interludes about his neighbors in Watts or about his experiences with the Ellington band, and an occasional profound conversation with Mingus favorites such as Fats Navarro. It is a portrait rather than a history, and a portrait of what Mingus's agent told Whitney Balliett was only "the superficial, the flashy" Mingus. The whole is framed as if it were spoken to Mingus's psychiatrist, allowing us, as with *Portnoy's Complaint*, to recognize the special pleading when it occurs. It is certainly the only autobiography I know of that begins with the disclaimer: "Some names in this work have been changed and some of the characters and incidents are fictitious." It says little about his music, but the little it says is worth contemplating, and no one has matched Mingus's

Charles Mingus *by Michael Ullman*

theory about his own nature: "In other words, I am three. One man stands forever in the middle, unconcerned, unmoved, watching, waiting to be allowed to express what he sees to the other two. The second man is like a frightened animal that attacks for fear of being attacked. Then there's an over-loving gentle person who lets people into the uttermost sacred temple of his being and he'll take insults and be trusting and sign contracts without reading them and get talked down to working cheap or for nothing, and when he realizes what's been done to him he feels like killing and destroying everything around him including himself for being so stupid."

Mingus was born in Watts in 1922; in his autobiography, he has enumerated the miseries of his childhood, describing how he was beaten for wetting his bed, accused unjustly while in kindergarten of looking up a little girl's skirt, how he split his head on a dresser and, more significantly, how he was confused about race—he was light-skinned but not white, and he couldn't understand either the white man's attitudes toward him or the equally dismaying hierarchy in the black community, where status was associated with light skin. He tells how he was taught to fear the Lord and to love music, including the gospel music he heard at his mother's church. There is a photograph of a four-year-old Mingus: he is perfectly bullet-shaped, chubby with sloping shoulders, fat hands, and a troubled, pouting face. He seems vulnerable, uncomprehending—guarded.

Mingus was eight when his father bought him a trombone. It was later traded for a cello. His first teacher was Mr. Arson: "In Watts, itinerant teachers—not always skillful or well educated in music themselves—traveled from door to door persuading colored families to buy lessons for their children. Mr. Arson . . . would teach anyone how to play anything even looking like a musical instrument that poor folks might beg or buy second-hand or on the installment plan. Mr. Arson by-passed the essentials that even the most talented child must master if he is ever to learn to read music well, and the parents, as usual, were paying for something their children were not getting." Arson taught Mingus to finger the cello and to play melodies but not to read music. The method turned out to be useful for a jazz musician who "listens to the sounds he's producing rather than making an intellectual transference from the score paper to the fingering process."

The young Mingus switched to bass on the advice of reedman Buddy Collette, who told him realistically: "You're black. You'll never make it in classical music no matter how good you are. You want to play, you gotta play a *Negro* instrument." Mingus's father bought him a bass, recognizing that music could provide his son with a way out of the ghetto. Soon Mingus was playing along with the radio and gathering advice from the active jazz community in Watts. Mingus got a sense of what he wanted to do with the bass when he heard a local hero, Red Callender, bow a version of "Body and Soul." Mingus told Britt Woodman, a trombonist who was part of an influential family band and who later starred with Ellington: "Britt, when I start really learning to play people will see me big, with a big bass but when I want it they'll hear a viola, my magic viola that plays high as a violin and low as a bass and gets rid of all the muddling undertones and produces a pizzicato sound with the clarity of Segovia!"

A black musician growing up in Watts could at least find teachers, often men and women whose own careers had been circumscribed by racial prejudice. Soon Mingus was studying composition with Lloyd Reese, a skillful leader who instructed Eric Dolphy and Dexter Gordon as well. Reese ran a rehearsal band on Sundays, and Mingus soon was playing with it, as well as with the school orchestra, and gigging with Buddy Collette before he was out of high school.

Mingus played with the Louis Armstrong and Lionel Hampton big bands in the '40s, and the latter recorded his composition, "Mingus Fingers," in 1947. But he was out of music, delivering mail, when he got his first big break: Red Norvo called him in 1950 to form the Red

Norvo trio, featuring Mingus and guitarist Tal Farlow. Mingus's strong time sense, his flexibility and his relatively advanced harmonic ideas were crucial to the trio's success, as was the variety of his techniques. A comment by Tal Farlow suggests that Mingus had achieved the sound he wanted: "Mingus got such a distinct sound. Each note would 'ting' with great clarity, no matter what the tempo. Unlike so many other bass players, he could separate one note from the other, no matter how fast we played. And he was so relaxed. I was always amazed, just watching his right hand. He played as if it were no effort at all, as if the bass were a guitar." The group recorded over twenty tunes for Savoy—none of them Mingus compositions— but it broke up on a sour note when Mingus was not allowed to play on television. The South wasn't ready to see a mixed group, sponsors felt, and Norvo wasn't willing to give up an appearance on national television.

Mingus had been recording his own compositions off and on since 1946, several times under the title "Baron Mingus": one company advertised "Charlie Baron Mingus Presents His Symphonic Airs." He formed his own Debut Records in 1952 and cut some "cool" sides for Savoy and Period, recordings that gradually introduced key features of Mingus's later performances: multiple lines in the horns, rhythmic intensity and variety, long melodic statements and brief, scrambling sections of free improvisation. Then in 1956 he began a crucial series of recordings for Atlantic with *Pithecanthropus Erectus* and *The Clown*, including the justly famous "Haitian Fight Song." The piece begins with an out-of-tempo blues chorus by Mingus, who falls into an insistent rhythm as his band enters *sotto voce*, building in intensity and volume until, with Mingus howling in the background, the ensemble drops out for Jimmy Knepper's solo. Then the tension starts to build again. It is a steamy but sophisticated work.

For most of the rest of his life Mingus was a bandleader, as creative in that role as he was in other ways. His widow, Sue Graham Mingus, told Michael Cuscuna on National Public Radio: "I used to listen to Charles's music night after night in clubs, and it was always different. He had that incredible energy—his music never got into a rut. If a sideman played a solo and got a lot of applause, he would yell at him, 'Don't do that again.' Ted Curson once said he thought it was because Mingus was jealous of the applause, but then he realized it wasn't that, but that Mingus didn't want him to repeat himself. Charles would not stand for anything going along haphazardly, without ideas. Charles as a bass player never had a sense that he was supposed to support the band. He would offer resistance to the band. If the ideas weren't flowing he would use every kind of technique—he'd change the beat, he'd change the key, he'd change the tune, he'd stop—to get the musicians going. If he thought nothing was happening, he would throw a bombshell, and that's what made him so consistently exciting. He would woo you or court you or humiliate you or fire you on the bandstand—there was no limit to his methods. Those who couldn't take it would quit, and those who stayed would grow. The music was all-important."

Mingus had economic and emotional problems throughout much of his life. One troubled night he talked a guard into allowing him into the psychiatric ward of Bellevue Hospital. Once inside he found it surprisingly difficult to get out. He was asked to write a letter describing why he would prefer to be treated by his personal psychologist. Under these circumstances he managed still to be humorous: point five of his letter is directed at a staff psychologist who had suggested that Mingus get a lobotomy: "Dr. Bonk keeps saying I am a failure. I did not come here to discuss my career or I would have brought a press agent." Mingus was released and, according to his autobiography, was thanked by his own Dr. Wallach for the nice things he said about private care.

Like Duke Ellington, Mingus wrote longer and more complicated compositions in the '60s and '70s. He heard the Juilliard String Quartet play Bartok and was temporarily depressed about his own work. As he told Nat Hentoff: "Hearing artists like this reminds me of my original goal but a thing called 'jazz' took me far off the path and I don't know if I'll ever get back. I am a good composer with great possibilities and I made an easy success through jazz but it wasn't really success—jazz has too many strangling qualities for a composer." But Mingus wasn't strangled by jazz, whose boundaries he helped to expand. Again in his autobiography, he talked about extended forms: "I've been using extended forms and prolonged chords for years and I wasn't the first with that either. I got ideas from Spanish and Arab music." Others got those ideas from Mingus.

It is clear that Mingus did not get all the recognition he deserved: a man with the musical skills of an Ellington, he hadn't Ellington's emotional reserve and balance, to say nothing of Ellington's slightly affected charm. Mingus was not always a comfortable character to be around. He spoke in barely comprehensible bursts: he had the fastest mumble in the business. He deeply resented racial prejudice, and he talked about what was on his mind. If he was, as he said, three men, one violent and frightened, and the second tender and trusting, we can be thankful for the third, Mingus the overseer, who organized the fear, the hurt, the rage and the love in his life, and who turned it into music.

At the end of *Beneath the Underdog*, Mingus is arguing about faith with the dying trumpeter Fats Navarro, trying to convince his despairing friend about the value of life. It seems a barely disguised conversation between Mingus and himself. Mingus did not save Fats Navarro, but he answered his own fears and doubts when he wrote: "My music is evidence of my soul's will to live." At the end of a recently issued piece, "New How Now How," one can hear the voice of the rarely satisfied Mingus signaling the engineer: "That was it, man. Did you hear that? That was *it*!" Of course he was right. He was open, shy, strong, funny, indignant, violent, often close to tears and a little crazy. His music was glorious. That *was* it. It still is.

DISCOGRAPHY

The following alphabetical list makes no attempt to be inclusive or definitive. I have recommended recordings that are valuable in themselves, and for the most part I have chosen albums that are generally available.

Artists House
Artists House's first release is impressive. Ornette Coleman's *Body Meta* offers five selections by Coleman and his "electrified" group. I miss the rich bass of Charlie Haden and the melodies of Ed Blackwell's drums, but it is rewarding to hear four new compositions by Coleman and a reprise of "European Echoes," previously recorded in 1965. Artists House 2 features recordings by the late Paul Desmond and a trio of Canadians: the selections were left over when Horizon assembled *The Paul Desmond Quartet Live* (A&M SP 850). Desmond's tone was one of the most affecting in jazz, restrained, cool, but pure and full. He exploited this sound easily, wobbling gracefully on a held note, tightening up on a high note, pushing from the belly for a suddenly expansive low note. Artists House 3 is a quartet date starring Thad Jones and Mel Lewis. Here they sound cohesive and alert, but not often inspired. The Hampton Hawes-Charlie Haden duets (Artists House 4) were among Hawes's last

recordings. Trained as a bebop pianist, Hawes had a deep lyrical streak submerged in the funky histrionics of his last Prestige recordings, but evident in compositions such as the waltz ballad "Sonora." In the masterpiece of this duet session, "As Long as There's Music," Haden's solo is an orderly lament based, one is astonished to observe, on the first four notes of the F Major scale. Guitarist Jim Hall and bassist Red Mitchell have recorded a set of duets (Artists House 5) that suggests an even greater intimacy than the Haden-Hawes collaboration. As Hall tells us in his notes, the two start a performance softly. Often they get softer. For me the highlight of this recording is the rendition of an urbane Mexican folksong, "Blue Dove." By contrast, the pair almost rock on Hall's humorous "Osaka Express." The record was taped at the New York nightclub Sweet Basil, where Hall has played with Red Mitchell.

(Artists House is located at 40 West 37th Street, New York, New York, 10018.)

Karl Berger

Listeners should still be able to find Don Cherry's *Symphony for Improvisers* (Blue Note 84247) with Berger appearing as a sideman. Berger's work with the Musica Ellectronica Viva is available on *United Patchwork* (Horo HDP 15-16). *Peace Church Concerts* (2-CMC 00101) is a poorly recorded live performance featuring Berger with Ing Rid's vocalizings, while *All Kinds of Time* presents Berger's duets with bassist Dave Holland (Sackville 3010). Its title cut features some elegant play with different time signatures and includes a section of swinging Milt Jackson mellowness, while "Perfect Love" is an attractive ballad. Berger plays piano as well as vibes on "Simplicity" and balafon on "Fragments." Dave Holland is inventive and responsive throughout, and the record's ready availability makes this the Berger album to start with. Berger rerecorded "Perfect Love" on the solo album *Interlude* (FMP 0460).

(Horo Records and Sackville Records are available

from Rounder Distribution, 186 Willow Street, Somerville, Mass., 02144. The address of FMP is Behaimstrasse 4, 1000 Berlin 10, West Germany. The Creative Music Studio receives mail at P.O. Box 671, Woodstock, New York, 12498.)

Ran Blake

The Blake-Lee collaboration on RCA is out of print, but New World Records has included "Laura" on its anthology of avant-garde and Third Stream jazz entitled *Mirage*. The Italian label Horo has issued two Blake solo albums, as has the French label Owl. *Wende* (Owl 05) contains only tunes written by Blake. These performances were used by Blake's publishers (Margun) as the basis of their edition of Blake compositions. Golden Crest has issued "Take One" and "Take Two" of eleven pieces—each album has a take of such tunes as Blake's "Biko," Theodorakis's "Vradiasi," Kern's "Ol' Man River" and, surprisingly, "Silent Night," which Blake turns into a convincing gospel number. Improvising Artists issued *Breakthru*, an album that received a five-star *Downbeat* review and that helped Blake revive his performing career. It contains a powerful version of the Charlie Parker blues, "Parker's Mood." More recent is Blake's Arista recording *Rapport*. Blake's "jazziest" album, it opens as Blake and Ricky Ford play "Alone Together" in a performance that shows the value of their decade of informal collaboration. It is remarkable for its wit: Ford sings "Alone" on the saxophone and stops, while Blake thuds on the piano; Ford plays the next three notes and is answered by another couple of chords. But when the second part of the theme is stated, Ford seems to float like a ballroom dancer over Blake's suddenly mellow foundation. The piece continues with some double-time passages until the last chorus, when the two slow to a crawl and sink to a whisper. Besides the five pieces with Ford, *Rapport* contains a duet with Anthony Braxton, who is surprisingly conservative and deferential on Blake's "Vanguard"; a version of "Wende" featuring Chris Connor, Blake's "favorite white singer"; and a performance of "Vradiasi" sung in Greek by Eleni Odoni. Its variety makes *Rapport* the first Blake album to buy.

Anthony Braxton

There are many Braxton albums readily available. I would begin with the Arista small group sessions— Arista 4064, 4032, 4101 and 4181. Braxton can be heard playing solo on the early double album, Delmark 420/1. That label also has Braxton's first album (Delmark DS 415 B); it features the Creative Construction Company, which can also be heard on Muse 5096/7. A later solo album is available as Inner City 1008. "Circle" can be heard on three two-record sets: ECM 1018/19, Blue Note LA 472-H2 and Blue Note LA 882-J2. I would not miss the duets with Max Roach on Black Saint (BSR 0024), or with synthesist Richard Teitelbaum on Arista 1037. Braxton's prize-winning big band album is Arista 4080, and his work for three orchestras is on Arista A3L 8900. One can hear him bounce off another Chicago-bred saxophonist, Joseph Jarman, on Delmark DS-428.

Betty Carter

The Carter-Ray Charles recording is not currently available, but some people should be able to find the double album Carter made with large groups in 1958 and 1960, rereleased as *What a Little Moonlight Can Do* (Impulse ASD-9321). **Inside Betty Carter**, with "This is Always" and "Open the Door," was last available as United Artists UAS 5639. There are listed three Roulette albums by Carter: each includes worthwhile examples of her dramatic style as well as an occasionally overindulgent solo. *Round Midnight* (Roulette SR-5001) is my favorite. Carter has issued two records on her own Bet-Car label. The support she receives from such musicians as Allen Gumbs and Buster Williams makes MK 1002 preferable to its predecessor.

(Bet-Car Records are available at 117 St. Felix Street, Brooklyn, New York, 11217.)

Doc Cheatham

One would like to hear Cheatham leading a group of sophisticated modern musicians, but as of yet no such record exists. Cheatham participated in "The Sound of Jazz" television production in 1957, and he solos once on the record made from that session (Columbia JCL 1098). He has several solos on a group of jam sessions organized by Buck Clayton (Chiaroscuro 132), and plays on one side of a peculiar record designed to unite modern and traditional musicians: Beaver Harris's *From Ragtime to No Time* (360 Degree Records 2001). Jezebel 102 is a two-record set with Cheatham accompanied by a trio of relatively uninteresting musicians. The package contains an interview with Cheatham and some family photos (Jezebel Records, 1233 Greenleaf Street, Allentown, Penn., 18102). Sackville 3013 is a set of duets with Cheatham and boogie-woogie pianist Sammy Price. One can hear "I Cover the Waterfront" and seven other classic tunes played by Cheatham's sextet on Classic Jazz 113.

Tommy Flanagan

To the 1957 album (Prestige 7632) has been added another recording with Elvin Jones (*Eclypso*, Inner City 3009); Jones played only brushes on the earlier recording—on the new one both Jones and Flanagan are more expansive. Pablo has issued the set dedicated to Strayhorn and Ellington (Pablo 2310-724) which includes a rollicking "A-Train" and a second version of the tune that helped make Ben Webster famous: "Chelsea Bridge." Pablo 2308 202 was recorded live at Montreux in 1977 and it is chiefly notable for two ballad medleys. Fantasy has issued a varied set, illustrating Flanagan's marvelous taste in choosing tunes and his flexibility in performing them. Thelonious Monk's odd, skipping "Friday the 13th" is introduced by some gospel chords, and the performance is marred only by some uncharacteristically stiff drumming by Jimmie Smith. Flanagan plays an even-toned electric piano on Dameron's "Good Bait" and on his own "Something

Borrowed, Something Blue" (GXY 5110). Flanagan can be heard in a supporting role on many albums, including the recently issued set by Coleman Hawkins, *The Real Thing* (Prestige P-24083). He accompanied Ella Fitzgerald on a recent live date (Pablo 2308 206). And he can be heard in a group of stimulating two-piano performances with Hank Jones on *Our Delights* (GXY 5113).

Dizzy Gillespie

The Smithsonian Institution has issued a valuable two-record set called *Dizzy Gillespie: The Development of an American Artist, 1940-46.* It contains several Gillespie solos with the Cab Calloway orchestra, and performances with the large groups of Les Hite, Lucky Millinder, Coleman Hawkins, Billy Eckstine, Boyd Raeburn and others, as well as nine of the most important Gillespie small group sessions. *In the Beginning* (Prestige P-24030) offers seven cuts with Charlie Parker, as well as sides by the Gillespie big band recorded in 1946. The famous Massey Hall concert of 1953 interestingly demonstrates the competitive spirit of Charlie Parker and his "worthy constituent" Gillespie (Prestige 24024). Arista has reissued the Dee-Gee sides, featuring the successful, confident Gillespie in the early '50s on bop classics such as "Ooh-Shoo-Be-Doo-Bee" (Arista Savoy SJL 2209). The mid-50s Gillespie can be heard in three double albums reissued by Verve and featuring other superstars: Roy Eldridge on Verve-2-2524; Stan Getz on Verve-2-2521; and Sonny Rollins and Stitt on Verve-2-2505. Gillespie hasn't slowed down in the '70s—some say he plays better than ever. I particularly recommend the Count Basie-Gillespie recordings issued as *The Gifted Ones* (Pablo 2310 833).

Dexter Gordon

Gordon's solo on "Lonesome Lover Blues" is available on *Billy Eckstine: Mister B. and the Band* (Arista Savoy 2214): the band includes Fats Navarro, Art Blakey and others, but is used primarily to back up

Eckstine's chesty vocals. Gordon can be heard in a jam session recorded in 1947 featuring Wardell Gray: *The Hunt* (Arista Savoy 2222). The performance is vibrant, the sound dim. One should start a Dexter Gordon collection with the indispensable *Savoy Sessions* (Arista Savoy 2211). These were recorded in the middle '40s, as were the three "tenor battles" with Teddy Edwards, recorded for Dial and now issued on Onyx 201. In the early '60s, Gordon made a series of striking albums for Blue Note, including *Our Man in Paris* with Bud Powell (BN 84146) and *Gettin' Around* (BN 84204). Unaccountably, I find the group he made for Prestige starting in 1969 less intense and satisfying. *Power* (Prestige P-24087), though, unites two of the best of these sessions. Gordon has been recording actively in the '70s, first with the Danish label Steeplechase, and then for Xanadu and Columbia. *Biting the Apple (Steeplechase 1080)* features Gordon with the estimable Barry Harris on piano. Of the CBS albums he has made so far, I prefer Gordon's *Manhattan Symphony* (JC 35608) for its version of "As Time Goes By" and for George Cables's rhythmically inventive piano. One final note: Xanadu 137, *Silver Blue*, features Gordon and Al Cohn in a duet on "On the Trail." They do more than salvage Grofe's banal though popular melody: this is, as the notes to the album tell us, "a small masterpiece."

Neal Hefti
"Wildroot" and "The Good Earth" can be found on *Woody Herman's Greatest Hits* (CBS CS 9291). Anyone who has heard the Count Basie band live is likely to have heard Hefti arrangements and compositions, but the original "Lil' Darlin'" is still available on *Fantail* (SR 42009). Later, speeded-up versions of this tune are best avoided. *Fantail* also contains "Whirly Bird," "The Kid from Red Bank," "Fantail" and "Splanky," all by Hefti. *Basie Plays Hefti* was last available as Emus 12003. Six Hefti compositions recorded by Basie in 1953 and 1954 are available on *Sixteen Men Swinging* (Verve 2-2517). Hefti's string arrangements for the late

Clifford Brown elicited some of Brown's warmest and most influential performances; they can be heard on Trip (TLP 5502).

Earl Hines

The Hines discography begins in the '20s, when the pianist joined Louis Armstrong for their "Hot Seven" recordings. This musical relationship culminated in the duet, "Weather Bird," recorded in 1928. Most of the Hines-Armstrong performances are available on Columbia 853. The Smithsonian has issued a two-record set of their 1928 collaborations (Smithsonian 2002). In the same year Hines recorded as a soloist eight of his compositions, including the famous "A Monday Date" and "Blues in Thirds." The performances are simply stunning (Milestone 2012). Hines's early work with the great New Orleans clarinetist Jimmy Noone was last available domestically as Decca 79235. Budd Johnson did many of the arrangements for the Earl Hines big band of the late '30s and '40s, including "Piano Man" (*The Grand Terrace Band*, RCA LPV 512). Bandstand 7115 has the vocals of the young Billy Eckstine behind the Hines band that included some bopsters. In the '50s, Hines was captured by Dixieland revivalists. His rediscovery in the '60s was the result of a concert organized by Stanley Dance at The New School; it was Hines's first solo concert. Since then he has recorded widely: *Quintessential Recording Session* (Chiaroscuro 101) is a new look at the compositions Hines first recorded in 1928. Hines recorded four albums of Duke Ellington material for Master Jazz; he is most inventive on the unfamiliar tunes of MJ 8132, but all four albums are worth looking for. Hines isn't usually thought of as a blues player, but his 1974 performances with Budd Johnson (Classic Jazz 129) are earthy enough, and the partnership with Johnson is entirely sympathetic.

Roland Kirk

"The Call" can be found on Argo 669. Mingus's *Oh Yeah!* is not currently listed, but Kirk's solo on "Devil

Woman" can be found on the Atlantic Anthology, *Charles Mingus: Passions of a Man* (Atlantic SD-3-600). *The Jaki Byard Experience* has been issued as part of *Pre-Rahsaan* (Prestige P-24080) and most of Kirk's playing with Elvin Jones has been reissued on *Kirk's Works* (Mercury EMS-2-411). *The Vibration Continues* (Atlantic SD 2-1003) is an anthology of Kirk's uneven performances in the years 1968-76, while *Bright Moments* (Atlantic SD 2-907) is a representative live recording: it includes several of Kirk's speeches and songs. *Mingus at Carnegie Hall* contains two of the long performances of Mingus's 1974 concert (Atlantic SD-1667).

Ray Mantilla

Max Roach's *Freedom Now Suite* is not available domestically, but Mantilla can be heard with Art Blakey on *In My Prime* (Timeless Muse TI 301). He plays, though not prominently, on Mingus's *Cuumbia and Jazz Fusion* (Atlantic SD-8801), contributes various percussive effects, including bird calls, on Richie Cole's *Alto Madness* (Muse 5155), and solos brilliantly on "Una Mas" and "Manteca" on Cedar Walton's *The Pentagon* (Inner City 6009). He appears on Joe Chambers's *The Almoravid* (Muse 5035) and on guitarist Karl Ratzer's *In Search of the Ghost* (Vanguard 79407). The "historic U.S.-Cuban musical exchange of 1977" has been issued as David Amram's *Havana/New York* (Flying Fish 057). *Mantilla* (Inner City 1052) is the percussionist's first album as a leader.

Ken McIntyre

The McIntyre-Dolphy date has been issued under the latter's name as part of *Fire Waltz* (Prestige P-24085); McIntyre provides the notes to the album, and talks further about his relationship with Dolphy. There are now five McIntyre albums on Steeplechase: *Hindsight* (SCS 1014) and *Open Horizon* (SCS 1049) with Kenny Drew; *Home* (SCS 1039) with Jaki Byard; and *Introducing the Vibrations*, featuring professional musicians that were McIntyre's students (SCS 1065). Steeplechase 1114 is a trio date with Hakim Jami on bass and Beaver Harris on drums. McIntyre can be heard briefly on Volumes 1 and 2 of the live Wildflower sessions (Douglas 7045, 7046).

(Steeplechase Records are available from Rounder Distribution, 186 Willow Street, Somerville, Mass., 02144.)

Marian McPartland

McPartland's early records for Savoy are unavailable, but she is determined to keep in print the records made for her Halcyon label. *Interplay* (Halcyon 100) has "New Orleans" as well as "Milestones" and "By the Time I Get to Phoenix." Halcyon 103 has McPartland's own tune "Ambiance" as well as the uptempo "Three Little Words." It features bassist Michael Moore and four of his compositions. *A Delicate Balance* (Halcyon 105) has "God Bless the Child" as well as the title tune, while Halcyon 109 is McPartland's tribute to Alec Wilder; she plays ten of his tunes. Halcyon 111 was recorded live at Haverford, and includes versions of "Send in the Clowns," "Killing Me Softly" and a Gershwin medley. Dixieland fans will want to hear the pianist's collaborations with ex-husband Jimmy (Halcyon 107, 114). McPartland has recorded a stirring album for Concord jazz: *From This Moment On* (CJ-86)—her interpretations of its ballads are ingenious and charming, and her musical relationship with bassist Brian Torff is consistently exciting.

(The address of Halcyon Records is 302 Clinton St., Bellmore, New York, 11710.)

Charles Mingus

In the notes of *Blues and Roots*, Mingus wrote: "At a concert or night club I call tunes in an *order* that I feel is right for the particular situation and what I'm trying to say in that situation. Each composition builds from the previous one, and the succession of compositions creates the statement I'm trying to make at that moment. The greatness of jazz is that it *is* an art of the moment." As these observations apply also to records, and particularly to Mingus's records, one can be grateful that Atlantic has reissued "Pithecanthropus Erectus," "Reincarnation of a Lovebird," "Haitian Fight Song," "Wednesday Night Prayer Meeting" and others on an anthology, while at the same time be disappointed that these masterpieces were not reissued in their original context and that the sessions were not rereleased *in toto.* Nevertheless, *Charles Mingus: Passions of a Man* (Atlantic SD-3-600) is the album with which one should begin a Mingus collection today. One can have the complete 1959 Columbia sessions only by finding *Better Git It In Your Soul* (Columbia G 30628) and *Nostalgia in Times Square* (Columbia JG 35717). *Charles Mingus Revaluation: The Impulse Years* contains the complete *Black Saint and the Sinner Lady,* a Mingus ballet score also available on Impulse 35, and selections from other Impulse sessions, including his warm and touching performance of "Mood Indigo." In the middle '60s, Mingus's concerts featured loose and lengthy renditions of his favorite compositions. Prestige has issued remnants of two such concerts, *The Great Concert of Charles Mingus* (Prestige 34001), an incompetently edited set that mixes the beginning of one night's performance of "So Long Eric" with the ending from the following evening and calls the whole "Goodbye Porkpie Hat," which is another piece entirely. But one can hear Eric Dolphy's work with Mingus on this record. *Let My Children Hear Music* (Columbia KC 31039) is a powerful recording from the '70s, brilliantly orchestrated and recorded, that has not received its share of attention, perhaps because several of the pieces are wholly composed. It is nevertheless one of the monuments of Mingus's later career. Mingus's last recorded solos are found on *Three or Four Shades of Blue* (Atlantic SD 1700), a set that shocked some fans by featuring two prolix electric guitarists, Larry Coryell and Philip Catherine. The Red Norvo trio dates featuring Mingus and Tal Farlow have been reissued on Arista Savoy SJL 2212.

Sam Rivers

Some readers will be able to find Rivers's albums for Impulse; he can be heard with various trios on *Hues* (Impulse ASD-9302), a recording whose titles at least might owe something to the days when Rivers would play "paintings." *Crystals* (ASD-9286) documents his recent big band techniques, from the dense multi-lines of "Exultation" to the good-natured funk of "Tranquility." Several live performances of 1972 and 1973 have been issued by Impulse on the double album *The Trio Sessions* (IA 9352/2). This issue includes the stirring blues sound of "Indigo," a less than two-minute cut that begins with a loose, rollicking drum and bass pattern and proceeds as Rivers plays blues tenor with easy skill and deep feeling. *Fuchsia Swing Song* (BLP 84184) with Jaki Byard and *Contours* (BLP 84206) with Freddie Hubbard are early recordings by Rivers that are still listed by Blue Note, but the company has dropped *Involution* (BN-LA 453-H2), with its 1967 sextet recording. Rivers can be heard as a sideman to Tony Williams (Blue Note 84180, 84216), to Don Pullen (Black Saint BSR 0004), and to Cecil Taylor (Prestige P-34003). He has recorded a series of stunning extended duets with bassist Dave Holland (Improvising Artists 373843, 373848), and in 1978 he recorded a varied set of impressive performances issued as *Wave* (Tomato 8002). *Wave* is the most attractive Rivers album now generally available.

Sonny Rollins

Rollins has demonstrated Tommy Flanagan's assertion that there is no one more musical than Sonny Rollins in a long series of recordings dating back to the early '50s. (His first recorded solos, made in 1949 with the Babs Gonzalez group, only faintly suggest what was to come.) Rollins's recordings with Bud Powell are on *The Amazing Bud Powell* (Blue Note 81503 and 81504). Rollins played as a sideman on some of the most satisfying Miles Davis dates, including *Conception* (Prestige 7744), where a faulty reed does not prevent the saxophonist from soloing skillfully on "Dig," "It's

Only a Paper Moon," and others. The session with "Vierd Blues" and Rollins's compositions "Oleo," "Doxy" and "Airegin" as well as two takes of "But Not For Me" can be found on Prestige 7847. The famous *Saxophone Colossus* session led by Rollins has been released in the double album Prestige P-24050. That collection is indispensable, as is *The Freedom Suite Plus* (Milestone 47007) and *Taking Care of Business* (Prestige 24082), with its furious up-tempo solos on "B. Swift" and "B. Quick" and its duet with John Coltrane on "Tenor Madness." *The Bridge* (RCA AFL1-0859), Rollins's 1962 recording with Jim Hall, is still listed; it includes a version of "God Bless the Child." RCA has not reissued domestically the other Rollins albums in its catalogue, but French RCA has, and the recordings include a set with trumpeter Don Cherry, best known for his work with Ornette Coleman (Victor 741091/092). *Sonny Rollins' Next Album* is Milestone MSP 9042. "Autumn Nocturne" is on Milestone M-55005, as is Donald Byrd. Milestone 9090 is even more recent Rollins, with a version of "My Ideal," in which Rollins is heard in duet with Larry Coryell, and a piece called "Disco Monk," which humorously alternates some measures of disco with a gentle elaboration of a wistful melody that deserves more serious treatment; if anything, it is the disco section that is closest to Monk, but the album as a whole suggests that Rollins has found the rhythm section he needs.

Horace Silver

Horace Silver can be heard on the famous "Walkin'" session of Miles Davis (*Tune Up*, Prestige 24077), with Sonny Rollins on Blue Note 81558, and as a member of the Art Blakey *Jazz Messengers* (Odyssey 32 16 0246). *The Best of Horace Silver* (Blue Note 84325) has Silver's most popular performances, including "Senor Blues," "The Preacher," "Doodlin," "Sister Sadie," "Filthy McNasty," and "The Tokyo Blues." Blue Note 84008 has "Cookin at the Continental," while "Song for My Father" is on Blue Note 84185. "Cape Verde Blues" is on Blue Note 84220, and the recent *Silver 'n*

Percussion is Blue Note LA 853-H. Blue Note has also issued an album of previously unreleased cuts from Horace Silver's most popular period—the late '50s and early '60s. It includes an attractive take of "Senor Blues" as well as a vocal version (Blue Note LA 945-H).

Joe Venuti

Stringing the Blues with Eddie Lang-Joe Venuti (CBS JC2L 24) is a collection of Lang and Venuti performances from the '20s to be supplemented by *Joe Venuti: 1927 to 1934* (Yazoo L-1062). *Jack Teagarden: King of the Blues Trombone* (Epic JSN 6044) has some early sessions with Venuti. The Italian label Joker has issued the complete Bix Beiderbecke; Venuti appears on Volumes 2, 3, 5, 6 and 14. Volume 14 has Venuti's off-color vocal contribution to "Barnacle Bill the Sailor"; listen carefully to the chorus. *The Golden Horn of Jack Teagarden* (MCA-227) has four performances by the Lang-Venuti All Star Orchestra, which includes Teagarden and Benny Goodman. Venuti recorded often in his last years: three times with Zoot Sims (Chiaroscuro 128, 134 and 142); twice with a talented group of Italians (Vanguard 79396, 79405); and also with Earl Hines (Chiaroscuro 145), Marian McPartland (Halcyon 112), Dave McKenna (Chiaroscuro 160), and George Barnes (Concord 14, 30). Nothing will have the impact of a live Venuti performance, but I prefer the more raucous of the recordings, and therefore recommend the Hines, Sims and McKenna dates, as well as the second performance with George Barnes, this one recorded live at the Concord Summer Festival.